American Power and World Order

THEMES FOR THE 21ST CENTURY

Titles in this series

American Power and World Order

CHRISTIAN REUS-SMIT

polity

First published in 2004 by Polity Press Ltd.

Reprinted 2005

Polity Press
65 Bridge Street
Cambridge CB2 1UR, UK

Polity Press
350 Main Street
Malden, MA 02148, USA

ISBN: 0-7456-3166-5 (hb)
ISBN: 0-7456-3167-3 (pb)

A catalogue record for this book is available from the British Library and has been applied for from the Library of Congress.

Library of Congress Cataloging-in-Publication Data

Reus-Smit, Christian, 1961–
   American power and world order / Christian Reus-Smit.
      p. cm. – (Themes for the 21st century)
Includes bibliographical references and index.
   ISBN 0-7456-3166-5 (hb : alk. paper) – ISBN 0-7456-3167-3 (pb : alk. paper)
1. United States–Foreign relations–2001-2. Unilateral acts (International law) 3. Balance of power. 4. World politics–1995-2005. I. Title. II. Series.

   E902.R48 2004
   327.73–dc22

                                                        2003017720

Typeset in 10.5 on 12 pt Plantin
by Kolam Information Services Pvt. Ltd, Pondicherry, India
Printed and bound in Great Britain by
Marston Book Services Limited, Oxford

For further information on Polity, visit our website: www.polity.co.uk

Contents

For Samát

'From little things big things grow.'
Paul Kelly

Preface

In the wake of terrorist attacks on September 11, 2001, the United States enjoyed high levels of international sympathy and support. The sheer scale and audacity of the attacks sent shock waves around the globe, eliciting expressions of outrage and commiseration from the most unlikely quarters. In the two years since the attacks, this support has dissipated, replaced by diplomatic contestation and widespread resentment. In many parts of the world the direction of American foreign policy is viewed with unease, even hostility. The Bush Administration has chalked up military victories in Afghanistan and Iraq, but it has lost much of the social capital America earned after the attacks, and it has ever so crudely chipped away at America's liberal identity in international relations. For many commentators, it is the 'muscularity' of the Bush Administration's approach to foreign policy that matters – stirred into action, and endowed with unparalleled material resources, the United States is supposedly willing and able to reshape world order to its will. This book grows out of a sense that international politics is not so simple, that muscularity does not necessarily produce desired political outcomes, and that squandering social capital and reputation depletes a state's political influence as surely as military or economic decline.

Its genesis lies in my ongoing conversations with an extraordinary group of friends and colleagues, most notably Mlada Bukovansky, Peter Christoff, Robyn Eckersley, Greg Fry, Stuart Harris, Paul Keal, Heather Rae, Peter Van Ness and Nicholas Wheeler. In the two years following the attacks of September 11, our conversations returned time and again to the nature of American power and its implications for global order. I became increasingly interested in what I see as a growing disjuncture between America's material resources and its ability to translate those into intended political outcomes. I found myself arguing that there is something deeply dysfunctional, even idealistic, about the understanding of power currently informing American foreign policy, and that this is already frustrating the United States' political influence. The intellectual satisfaction I gained from testing these ideas with friends and colleagues encouraged me to put fingers to keyboard, to write a small essay-style book for a general as well as an academic readership. The finished product has benefited greatly from critical feedback, and I thank all of those named above for their efforts in reading parts or all of the manuscript.

Over the past year I have tested bits of the argument before a range of audiences, including the Biennial Air Power Convention, the College of Defence and Strategic Studies, seminars at the Commonwealth Attorney General's Department, my Department's short course for the Australian Department of Foreign Affairs and Trade, and the Department of International Relations Seminar Series at the Australian National University. Students in my graduate seminar on International Relations Theory heard parts of the argument as it unfolded, and two of my Ph.D. students, Joel Quirk and Sarah Graham, provided challenging feedback and much appreciated encouragement. Tom Gregg, my former student and running companion, heard me rehearse each step of the argument as we did our morning runs through the trails of O'Connor Ridge and Black Mountain, always managing to test me with a hard question just as we started up a big hill.

Louise Knight, my editor at Polity, has supported the project enthusiastically from the outset, offering patient, sage advice at crucial junctures. Mary-Louise Hickey, my Department's research officer, ploughed through the manuscript several times, providing critical feedback and much-needed assistance with formatting and proofreading. Michelle Burgis conducted most of the research assistance for the project, and without her help the project would never have been completed in such a short time frame.

The book took form during a momentous time in my life. Just before I started writing, Heather and I travelled to Thailand to adopt our new son, Samát. I struggle for words to describe what this has meant to me, and can only clumsily say that there is something deeply enriching about simultaneously coming to love a new little person, discovering unknown sides to oneself, developing new aspects of one's marriage, and thinking hard about challenging dimensions of the surrounding world. I thank Heather and Sam for giving me this and ever so much more.

Finally, a word of condolence. As I was in the final stage of revising the manuscript I learnt of the sudden, unexpected death of Professor Paul Hirst, renowned social and political theorist and scholar of globalization. Unbeknown to me, Polity had asked Paul to serve as a reader for the book, but sadly he was unable to complete the report before his death. I have long admired Paul's scholarship, but I never had the pleasure of meeting him. There is no doubt that his comments on the manuscript would have been insightful and immensely helpful, and the arguments of the book would certainly have been that much sharper for his thoughts.

Chris Reus-Smit
Canberra, August 2003

Introduction

One of the defining features of international relations at the beginning of the twenty-first century is the simple fact of America's material preponderance. The United States has greater economic and military resources than any other state in history, and dwarfs its nearest competitors by a substantial margin. The size of its military forces and level of military expenditure is unmatched, while its economy is the largest and most dynamic in the world, spurred on by its leadership in advanced information and communications technologies. So preponderant is the United States, that even the most sober commentators have prefaced their remarks by declaring that 'Never since Rome has one country so nearly dominated the world'.[1]

Yet despite this material preponderance, a second feature of contemporary international relations stands out – Washington's frustrated struggle to translate its material resources into desired political outcomes. Stephen Brooks and William Wohlforth claim that 'the sources of American strength are so varied and so durable that US foreign policy today operates in the realm of choice rather than necessity to a greater degree than any other power in modern history'. 'Now and for the foreseeable future,' they argue, 'the United States will have immense power resources it can bring to bear to force or entice others to do its bidding on a case-by-case basis.'[2]

The problem is that America's attempts to flex its muscle and impose its will are being repeatedly frustrated. In March 2003 the United States suffered its worst diplomatic defeat in fifty years when it failed to convince a 'moral majority' of the United Nations Security Council that force was needed to disarm Saddam Hussein. Its subsequent military victory in Iraq achieved the immediate, thinly veiled goal of regime change, but at substantial cost to America's international prestige and moral standing. The Bush Administration's 'road map for peace' in the Middle East, which regime change in Iraq was meant to facilitate, seems no closer to realization than previous initiatives. The 'war against terrorism' has yielded regime change in Afghanistan and Iraq but not greater American security, as the attacks in Riyadh and Morocco sadly indicate. Washington has waged vigorous campaigns against the International Criminal Court and the Kyoto Protocol on global warming, but the Court is now established, with a growing list of member states, and the Protocol is likely to come into effect within a year.[3] Despite the Bush Administration's wavering on participation in the renegotiation of the 1988 Basle Capital Adequacy accord, European states are likely to proceed on their own, with potentially significant costs for American banks operating in Europe. On a broad range of issues, a widening gulf is emerging between the United States and its principal European allies, and the much-vaunted international coalition against terrorism binds a disparate group of states by only the thinnest strand of common interest.

The existence of a superpower with such extraordinary material preponderance, yet frustrated political influence, constitutes a central paradox of our time. At the most fundamental level, it raises profound questions about the nature of power in contemporary global politics. If the sole remaining superpower cannot translate its material resources into desired political outcomes unproblematically, what are the sources of international power? Clearly, power must flow from more than the barrel of a gun or the depths of a purse. Fathoming the nature of power in the contemporary world is crucially important for the future of world order. If policy-makers in Washington misunderstand the nature and limits of American power, as too many indicators suggest, miscalculation and misadventure will become the norm, with serious risks for international peace and security, as well as the successful prosecution of American national interests. If other states similarly misunderstand the nature of power, and unreflectively equate material might with successful political influence, they will either encourage destabilizing American policies and practices through bandwagoning, or spur accelerated military and strategic competition through balancing – or do both simultaneously.

This book is a critical reflection on the paradox of American power and its implications for global order and justice at the beginning of the twenty-first century. It focuses on the neo-conservative ideas about American power and hegemony that inform the foreign and defence policies of the Administration of President George W. Bush. According to these ideas, America's material preponderance and universal values give Washington the means and right to reshape world order. In the following pages I argue that this view of power is deeply mistaken and can only lead to dysfunctional policies and practices. Material resources are not irrelevant to power, and America's material preponderance cannot be denied or understated. Similarly, rhetorical appeals to freedom and liberty have an undeniable universal ring to them. Yet material resources and universalist rhetoric do not automatically and unproblematically produce political influence. Effective influence depends on more than coercion, bribery or the threat of non-participation; it depends on the degree to which a state's policies and practices are deemed legitimate by other states and by international public opinion. The failure of neo-conservative policy-makers and commentators to grasp the social nature of power threatens to undermine the effective prosecution of American interests, while ever so gradually weakening the fabric of international society.

Chapter 1 traces the rise of the neo-conservative discourse on American power and its articulation in the Bush Administration's grand strategy. During the 1990s, a diverse yet bounded debate flourished in the United States about America's role in a new world order, a debate that threw up ideas of unipolarity, multipolarity, democratic peace, the end of history, the clash of civilizations, and more. It was from this debate that the neo-conservative view of American power emerged, a genesis marked by the artful co-opting of potentially antithetical ideas. Its rise to prominence was less a victory in the marketplace of ideas, however, than an example of the contingency of history. Unilateralist undercurrents in American foreign policy surfaced in the Clinton Administration's rhetoric of the United States as the 'indispensable nation', and in its circumvention of the Security Council in the Kosovo campaign. The two events that allowed neo-conservatives to turn these undercurrents into a tidal shift were the Supreme Court handing George W. Bush the 2000 presidential election and the catalytic events of September 11 in 2001. The crucial thing for our purposes is that the newly ascendant and empowered doctrine of power is decidedly idealist, even if it is often clothed in the garb of hard-headed realism. It is a curious and potentially dangerous mixture of material self-confidence, universalizing self-interest and unreflective faith in America's transformative capacities, one that overstates the salience of material resources, ignores the social bases of power and denies the complexities of global political life.

Chapter 2 addresses the nature of power in international relations. Underlying the Bush Doctrine is a theory of power, one that is possessive, primarily material, subjective and decidedly non-social. This view of power suffers from three potentially fatal flaws. To begin with, it assumes that power resources and political influence exist in a relationship of simple causality, with material preponderance unproblematically spawning political influence. But this assumption sits uncomfortably with reality, such as the degree of diplomatic frustration currently experienced by the United States, despite its unparalleled material attributes. At best there is an attenuated relationship between material endowments and the ability to control political outcomes, but there is little evidence that the Bush Administration appreciates this. The second flaw concerns the neo-conservative view of legitimacy. Legitimacy is a social phenomenon; an actor or action is not legitimate unless other members of society deem it so. Yet the Bush Administration seems to think that the legitimacy of the United States and its foreign policy depends on nothing more than the universality of its national interests. It fails to understand that one can assert one's legitimacy as loudly as one likes, but it is meaningless if others do not agree. The final flaw relates to the assumed cultural magnetism of the United States, a frequently cited pillar of American 'soft' power. The problem here is not that people around the world don't covet Levi jeans, Disneyland and Ivy League education – many clearly do. The problem is that neo-conservatives assume that because people covet these things they will uncritically accept America's global political tutelage, which is almost certainly untrue. Given these flaws in the neo-conservative view of power, I go on to outline an alternative, social conception of power, one that stresses the importance of authority, legitimacy and institutions for sustainable political influence. This view of power exposes the central paradox of hegemony: that stable, enduring leadership requires power to be socially embedded, and that unilateral action can be socially corrosive, with implications for both the preponderant state and world order.

If the neo-conservative understanding of power is logically flawed, it is also incompatible with the basic structures and processes of contemporary world politics. Neo-conservative policy-makers and commentators frequently draw an analogy between the world today and the golden age of American power following the Second World War. Then, as now, America was materially predominant, the world faced grave threats and challenges, and the unwavering exercise of American power created a more peaceful and prosperous world order. What this misses, of course, is that although America was materially predominant immediately after 1945, and enjoys such a position again today, the world in which it must now navigate its way is radically different. Chapter 3 provides a systematic, though not exhaustive, comparison of the world today with that of fifty years ago. It focuses on five points of structural difference: the level of security dependence and common threat perception among the great powers, the nature of international economic association, the density of institutionalization, the relative autonomy of the society of states and the diffusion of normative agency. In each of these areas, the two worlds differ markedly, and it will be fundamentally more difficult for American policy-makers to establish hegemony in today's world than it was five decades ago. This difficulty is exacerbated by the global consolidation of two phenomena: the system of sovereign states, and liberal market economics. These consolidations have produced a triad of destabilizing side-effects: the 'domestication' of war, the persistent maldistribution of global wealth and the crisis in the global ecosystem. Together, these pose profound challenges for American leadership and effective global governance.

It is taken as axiomatic by neo-conservatives that the Bush Administration's grand strategy is inherently and unproblematically just. But how should we think about the ethics of its revisionist project of hegemonic renewal? Chapter 4 assesses existing arguments about the moral bases of hegemony, concentrating on the following propositions: that might is right; might is right if it delivers international public goods; might is right if it serves cosmopolitan ends; might is right if it is liberal; and might is never right. I reject the first and last of these, and suggest that the challenge is to integrate the remaining three positions, each of which contain kernels of wisdom. I propose a pragmatic synthesis which gives normative priority to the satisfaction of basic human rights, but prudential priority to institutionally governed change. From this synthesis, I distil four interdependent rules of thumb for assessing the ethics of the Bush Doctrine: a revisionist grand strategy might be ethically justifiable (1) if it serves the satisfaction of basic human rights; (2) if it is governed by the procedural and substantive rules of international society; (3) if it helps provide international public goods, as long as these are compatible with rules 1 and 2; and (4) if primary international rules are violated only to prevent supreme humanitarian emergencies. Sadly, though perhaps not unexpectedly, the Bush Administration's grand strategy does not rate well against these rules. This is not because of inconsistent rhetoric, though. The Administration upholds cosmopolitan-sounding values, but these are contradicted by other aspects of its policies and practices.

It expresses support for international institutions, but this is nullified by its penchant for the diplomacy of ultimatum and exit. It veils its military interventions in humanitarian language, but its inconsistency, selectivity and barely submerged self-interest do little to discourage cynicism.

The final chapter brings the discussion to a close by considering the implications of the Bush Administration's dysfunctional understanding of American power for the pursuit of American interests and the future of global order. I argue that viewing power as possessive, primarily material, subjective and non-social leaves Washington with an impoverished repertoire of diplomatic techniques, or more appropriately 'anti-diplomatic' techniques. Coercion, bribery and exit from institutions are privileged, but communication, negotiation and cooperation atrophy. Herein lies the ultimate source of Washington's diplomatic frustrations – in today's highly complex global order, coercion, bribery and exit are sub-optimal means of achieving one's interests, even for a materially predominant state. I illustrate the limits of these techniques by briefly examining Washington's diplomatic defeat in the United Nations over war with Iraq. Such techniques are not only damaging to American interests, though; they are also threatening the fabric of international society and the future of global order. I conclude the chapter by positing four possible consequences for the international system if American policy does not change course in the short to medium term: (1) the weakening of some international institutions, the novel evolution of others and the construction of new extra-American regimes; (2) the increased frequency of 'institutional balancing' between states; (3) the growing disenchantment and activism of local and global civil-society actors; and (4) the continuing failure to address the domestication of war, the persistent maldistribution of global wealth and the crisis in the global ecosystem.

Before proceeding, four things should be noted. First, this is a book about a set of ideas, their inherent illogic and their incompatibility with contemporary global structures, processes and challenges. It does not provide detailed analyses of particular policy initiatives taken by the Bush Administration. It assumes, quite confidently in this case, that foundational beliefs, such as the Administration's view of power, provide the ideational framework in which particular policy initiatives are defined and prosecuted. This does not mean that individual policies and their attendant practices are direct reflections of these beliefs; the vagaries of personality, bureaucracy, domestic politics and circumstance militate against this. But, as Max Weber famously argued, foundational beliefs work like 'switchmen', determining the tracks along which action moves.[4]

Second, this is a book about a particular American power-projection strategy, the one articulated by contemporary neo-conservative thinkers and embodied in the Bush Administration's grand strategy. It does not provide a narrative or analytical history of American power-projection policies in general. Such histories are beyond the scope of a small book. But, more importantly, the Bush Administration's strategy is worthy of analysis in its own right. Most studies of hegemony in international relations have focused on the cases of nineteenth-century Britain and post-1945 United States, both of which are cases of a hegemon sponsoring the creation of international institutions in relatively underdeveloped institutional environments. The Bush Administration's grand strategy is interesting because it is a revisionist project of hegemonic renewal, pursued by a materially preponderant state, in a densely institutionalized global order. Moreover, it entails a willingness on the part of the Administration to dismantle institutions that might curtail its freedom of action, even when other members of international society remain strongly committed to those institutions. This is unique, both historically and in terms of the threats it poses to American national interests and global order.

Third, my characterization of the Bush Doctrine as a project of hegemonic renewal reflects the more general view of hegemony that informs the following discussion. My understanding of hegemony is relatively conventional. A state is hegemonic when it has the capacity to define the rules of international society, or, as Robert Keohane and Joseph Nye put it, 'when it is powerful enough to maintain the essential rules governing interstate relations, and [is] willing to do so'.[5] As chapter 2 explains, I reject the realist proposition that such power can derive from material resources alone – consent and legitimacy are crucially important. In this sense, my understanding has much in common with that advanced by Gramscian scholars. However, I am uncomfortable with their idea that the hegemony of a dominant state necessarily stands in a near symbiotic relationship with dominant ideological and economic structures and processes. It encourages a totalizing view of power, one that too readily accepts the commonality of power and interest between the American state and global capital, and uncritically assumes that globalized 'American' cultural artefacts, such as Coke and Nike, are American power resources. From the 'thin Gramscian' perspective advanced here, the United States was a hegemon between 1945 and the early 1970s, and since then its capacity to define the rules of international society has declined. The Reagan Administration engaged in a major project of hegemonic renewal in the early 1980s, and many attribute the end of the Cold War to this exercise in power politics. For neo-conservatives, though, the project lost momentum with the end of the Cold War, and the Bush Doctrine must be seen as an attempt by 'neo-Reaganites' to use America's position of material preponderance to re-establish US hegemony in the twenty-first century.

Finally, although the book focuses on the power-projection policies embodied in the Bush Administration's grand strategy, its subject matter is broader than this. Focusing on the Bush strategy is justified by its attendant dangers, but it also serves as a useful site in which to examine a series of deeper issues, such as the nature of power, the challenges of contemporary global governance, and the troublesome relationship between ethics and power in an interdependent yet diverse world. The idea that power stems from more than material resources – that it is inherently relational, institutional and social – is of general applicability. So too is the idea that even the most powerful states cannot escape the profound global challenges wrought by the globalization of the state system and liberal market economics. Similarly, thinking systematically about the ethics of preponderant power is a challenge we will need to confront long after the Bush Administration is gone. If the arguments advanced here are correct, the dysfunctional nature of the Administration's approach to global politics may well rebound to its detriment. But America's material preponderance is likely to remain for some time, giving questions of hegemony, governance and ethics in world politics enduring salience.

1

The Idealism of Preponderance

Forty years of Cold War between the United States and the Soviet Union produced a canon of received wisdom about the nature and limits of American and Soviet power, the parameters of national and international security, and the structure and dynamics of the international system. The bipolar distribution of power was taken for granted. Leading scholars saw it as the principal cause of a 'long peace' among the great powers, and they confidently predicted its persistence well into the twenty-first century.[1] Mutual deterrence and the preservation of alliances and spheres of influence were seen as essential to national and international security. International institutions, such as the United Nations, were considered marginal to the main game of superpower politics. The United States was recognized as the most powerful state, but even the most conservative commentators and policy-makers saw it as fundamentally constrained by the fact of bipolarity.

The dramatic end to the Cold War pulled the rug out from beneath these assumptions. Although some commentators were slow to admit it, the bipolar order was finished – the Soviet Union had relinquished control over Eastern Europe, the Velvet Revolutions had displaced the region's communist rulers and the Soviet Union had eventually voted itself out of existence. The distribution of international power was fundamentally altered, raising multiple questions about the sources of change, the meaning and principal contours of such change, and about the 'new world order' that would emerge. Not surprisingly, American scholars proffered a bewildering array of competing answers to these questions, particularly concerning the implications for the United States as the sole surviving superpower. Proclamations of a 'unipolar moment' vied with claims of a new multipolarity. Ideas of 'the end of history' were challenged by fears of a 'clash of civilizations'. And concerns about competition from rising powers, such as Japan, were countered by arguments about America's enduring 'soft power'.

A decade later, and two years after the tragic events of September 11, 2001, this contested terrain of ideas has generated a new, ascendant discourse of American power and global order, most ardently expressed in the policy prescriptions of the present Bush Administration. This new discourse weaves together four core themes: a celebration of America's unparalleled material preponderance; a quasi-religious belief in the universality of American values and priorities; an unfettered confidence in Washington's capacity to translate its material resources into intended outcomes in the international arena; and an abiding sense of threat, sufficient to justify institutional adjustment at home and pre-emptive action abroad. These ideas were catalysed by the events of September 11, but they are rooted in the 1990s neo-conservative discourse on American power and international relations. In the early 1990s, this discourse was but one voice in a cacophony of voices, but a decade later it is ascendant. Its ascendance, however, has been syncretic; ideas of unipolarity and American primacy have been fused into a curious ideological amalgam with those of democratic peace, the end of history, a clash of civilizations, and more.

This chapter traces, in a necessarily brief fashion, the rise to prominence of this new discourse of American power and world order, which I term 'the idealism of preponderance'. After surveying the main characteristics of the Cold War's end, and the near total failure of mainstream scholars and commentators to anticipate such a momentous change, I discuss in greater detail the struggle for understanding it engendered within the United States. My focus then turns to a strand of neo-conservative thought that eventually emerged from the margins to define the parameters of George W. Bush's national security doctrine. For John Lewis Gaddis, the dean of Cold War history, this doctrine could well be 'the most important reformulation of US grand strategy in over half a century'.[2] Its genesis, however, was marked by two features: it evolved into a fully fledged ideology of American power by conscripting and taming other potentially antithetical ideas; and it grew out of a bounded realm of American debate, one noted as much for its silences, blind spots and cognitive refusals as its apparent diversity.

The shock of the new

Throughout the 1980s, scholarly debate about international relations in the United States was dominated by an internecine debate between neorealists and neoliberals, neither of which were especially well equipped to comprehend or explain major transformations in the international system. Neoliberals stressed the role that institutions could play in facilitating coexistence and managing cooperation problems between states, arguing that it is often rational for self-interested actors to prefer cooperation over conflict, and that institutions could facilitate this.[3] Buried within these ideas was a conception of incremental change, the kind of change that occurs through structured cooperation and reciprocal exchange. But neoliberalism had little to say about epochal, systemic changes, such as the end of the Cold War. Neorealists were primarily concerned with understanding continuity in world politics, but in contrast to their neoliberal counterparts they did have an argument about systemic change. Change was said to occur when there was a major shift in the international balance of power, from bipolarity to multipolarity or unipolarity. Such changes were driven by the rise and decline of great powers, which was in turn driven by the struggle for relative power.[4] The only problem was that neorealists considered bipolarity the most stable of all balances of power, and in the 1980s they failed to see any major shifts in the balance of power or any potential challengers for supremacy on the horizon. China was still considered a developing nation, Japan was thought to lack the requisite military power, Europe was not sufficiently unified, and no one seriously imagined that the Soviet Union would give up the race.[5]

At a purely descriptive level, the end of the Cold War seemed to be an instance of systemic change as neorealists understood it. Robert Gilpin, in his classic study of war and change, defined systemic change as 'the rise and decline of dominant states or empires that govern the particular international system'.[6] From this perspective, the Cold War's end fitted neatly within the neorealist conceptual frame. Yet there was much about this epochal change that this frame could not accommodate. Gilpin and others held that 'the essence of systemic change involves the replacement of a declining power by a rising dominant power'.[7] The end of the Cold War, however, involved not a rising power, but a retrenching one. While neorealists assume that states seek survival above all else, the Soviet

Union not only relinquished its empire, it voluntarily dissolved into its constituent republics. After the fact, realists argue that the Reagan Administration forced these changes through its renewed arms offensive and invigorated ideological crusade. But this asks us to ignore some of the most interesting and salient features of this change, such as the roots of Mikhail Gorbachev's 'new thinking' in the alternative trans-European security discourse of the 1980s, the role of Western European peace movements and Eastern European dissidents – from Solidarity to Charter 77 – in undercutting the legitimacy of the Cold War's political and military structures, the persistence of detente between Europe and the Soviet Union throughout the second Cold War, and, finally, Ronald Reagan's own 'road to Damascus' conversion from confrontation to constructive engagement.

Convinced of continuity in world politics, and comprehending change only in terms of rising or falling hegemons, neorealists were blind to these ideational developments and international social forces. In 1979, Kenneth Waltz predicted that the bipolar order would persist well into the twenty-first century, and a year later Gilpin surveyed factors that might destabilize such an order, concluding that 'none of these destabilizing developments appears immanent in the contemporary world [1980], at least in the immediate future'.[8] After the event, realist policy-makers were quick to claim responsibility.[9] As Dan Deudney and John Ikenberry observed, though, the 'Cold War's end was a baby that arrived unexpectedly, but a long line of those claiming paternity has quickly formed'.[10] For their part, realist scholars have responded by abandoning the stark precepts of neorealism in favour of a return to richer strands of classical realist thought, which they claim provides a compelling *post hoc* explanation for the Cold War's demise.[11] This strategy has been strongly criticized, however, for stretching realism to include ideas about world politics pillaged from other traditions of thought.[12]

While it is widely held that the end of the Cold War caught all commentators unaware, there were some who were not so surprised. In 1980 the Hungarian intellectual and dissident Ferenc Feher wrote that it 'is unavoidable that during the eighties in certain countries open social conflict will break out in order to bring about a modicum of political pluralism . . . [T]here is little doubt in our mind that Poland is again likely to have the dubious distinction of becoming a world-historical nation: the centre of the gathering storm.'[13] Two years later, the British historian and peace activist Edward P. Thompson predicted that:

> we may now be living . . . through episodes as significant as any known in the human record. . . . There would not be decades of detente, as the glaciers slowly melt. There would be rapid and unpredictable changes: nations would become unglued from their alliances; there would be sharp conflicts within nations; there would be successive risks. We could roll up the map of the Cold War, and travel without maps for a while.[14]

These writers foresaw what mainstream American commentators could not because they were attuned to aspects of political life occluded by realist lenses, particularly the fact that the Cold War was in essence a structure of domination, the social legitimacy of which was fast eroding.[15]

The struggle for understanding

The dramatic conclusion to the Cold War sparked a wave of new imaginings about the nature and future of world politics in general, and about the place and role of the United States in particular. What had been a stiflingly narrow mainstream discourse on international relations gave way to a much more diverse, if bounded, debate. As Greg Fry and Jacinta O'Hagan observe in their definitive study of this debate, each of the new contending images 'represents a different position on the issue of what entities and forces matter in world politics, on the possibilities of peace and war, about the moral basis of global order, about how "security" is to be viewed, and about whether the world should be seen as one polity, or two, or many'.[16] For some authors, fundamental, world-transforming shifts were occurring in the underlying foundations of world politics; for others, we were witnessing yet another turn in the eternal cycle of recurrence and repetition that characterizes relations among sovereign states. This debate can be carved up in any number of ways, but the most apparent divide lies between the euphoric and the anxious, the optimistic and pessimistic, the brave new worlders and the harbingers of a more dangerous, 'primordial' future.

Euphoria

There was no equivalent to VE or VJ day to mark formally the cessation of Cold War hostilities. The fall of the Berlin Wall has become symbolic of this end, but the full import and magnitude of the process unfolded over several years, from 1989 to 1992. This lack of a victorious moment, however, did not dampen victorious sentiment, particularly in the United States. The end of the Cold War was cast variously as a victory for American policy, for the American system of government and economic life, for capitalism and democracy, for a particular kind of civilization, and for that amorphous community called 'the West'.

More sober and reflective voices argued that in fact 'We all lost the Cold War',[17] but for many it seemed patently obvious that, in the last of the twentieth century's great contests between contending political and economic systems, one superpower remained standing and one system prevailed, vibrant and expanding.

For some, the simple fact of there being a sole remaining superpower defined the essence of the victory. This was the 'unipolar moment'. Charles Krauthammer proclaimed in a 1990 *Foreign Affairs* article that there 'is but one first-rate power and no prospect in the immediate future of any power to rival it'.[18] So pre-eminent was the United States in the crucial military, diplomatic, political and economic fields, that it could 'be a decisive player in whatever part of the world it chooses to involve itself'.[19] Neo-conservatives like Krauthammer challenged Americans to recognize and embrace this new-found supremacy. Multipolarity was a myth, and multilateralism dangerous nonsense. 'The United Nations,' Krauthammer wrote, 'is guarantor of nothing. Except in a formal sense, it can hardly be said to exist at all.'[20] The only alternative was for the United States to have 'the strength and will to lead a unipolar world, unashamedly laying down the rules of world order and being prepared to enforce them'.[21] This was essential because, despite the victory over the Soviet Union, the world was likely to become more rather than less dangerous. 'Weapon states' were likely to arise, characterized by authoritarian rule and anti-Western sentiment, and armed with weapons of mass destruction. Iraq was considered the prototype of such a state, and North Korea one in the making.

While not denying the unipolar moment, another strand of victorious thinking stressed the victory of liberal democracy as an ideology and form of governance. For Francis Fukuyama, the Cold War's end marked nothing less than the end of history.[22] Not history in the sense of the ongoing parade of life, death, love and drama, but history understood as a process of social and political evolution driven by a dialectical clash of ideologies. After more than two centuries of often violent competition, liberal democracy had triumphed over hereditary monarchy, fascism and then communism. More than this, though, Fukuyama argued that 'while earlier forms of government were characterized by grave defects and irrationalities that led to their eventual collapse, liberal democracy was ultimately free from such fundamental internal contradictions'.[23] This victory of liberal democracy – which encompassed the triumph of capitalism – was ultimately due to the inherent dynamics of modern science, with its impact on technology and economic life, and to the innate human struggle for recognition, which only liberal democracy could satisfy.[24] Fukuyama predicted that for the foreseeable future the world would be divided into an expanding 'post-historical' realm of liberal democracies and a contracting 'historical' realm of authoritarian states, almost exclusively in the developing world. In the first of these worlds, power politics would be replaced by largely peaceful forms of economic competition; in the second, power politics would continue, fuelled by religious, national and ideological conflicts. For the most part, these worlds would 'maintain parallel but separate existences', but control over oil, problems of immigration and the spread of dangerous high technologies would give the liberal democracies common cause to protect themselves against threats emanating from those states still mired in history.[25]

Integral to Fukuyama's thesis was a set of ideas about how democratic states relate to one another, ideas that were being vigorously promoted by a group of newly empowered neo-Kantian thinkers. Since the end of the Cold War it has become almost a truism that democracies do not fight wars with each other, even if they confront perceived dictatorships with some enthusiasm. Throughout the post-1945 period, Immanuel Kant was seen as a naive idealist who had little if anything of substance to say about world politics. Yet one of his central insights – that 'republics' are unlikely to go to war with one another – was now embraced in the United States as a virtual law of international relations. Scholars went to elaborate empirical lengths to demonstrate the historical veracity of this law,[26] and the Clinton Administration, re-embracing long-neglected Wilsonian strands in American foreign policy, used it to justify the central policy principle that if you want to preserve world peace, spread democracy.[27] Several reasons were advanced as to why democracies might have such peaceful inclinations, including their mutual recognition of each other as legitimate, the fact that those who bear the costs of war have some say in its declaration, and the calming effects of international trade and interdependence. The crucial thing was that the end of the Cold War was hailed by those advancing these arguments as the 'democratic moment', in which 'the world [sic] people have come, through bitter experience, to a new appreciation of political freedom and constitutionalism as ends in themselves'.[28] The opportunity for the United States was clear. 'By promoting democracy abroad, the United States can help bring into being for the first time in history a world composed mainly of stable democracies.'[29]

The final strand of victorious discourse brought together elements of each of the above imaginings. Its roots lay in 1980s debates about America's impending hegemonic decline. A series of major works had suggested that the United States was experiencing serious imperial overstretch, in which the costs of empire were outpacing its economic capacity to meet those costs. Meanwhile, less encumbered great powers were rising to challenge

America's position, setting in train yet another grand historical cycle of hegemonic rise and decline.[30] The end of the Cold War coincided with the articulation of a highly influential neoliberal response to this thesis. To be sure, America would never again have the relative power it enjoyed at the end of the Second World War, a situation attributable as much to the utter devastation and exhaustion of the other great powers as to America's own attributes. But this did not mean that American primacy was in question. In addition to its unparalleled military and economic resources, the United States was also said to have something called 'soft' or 'co-optive' power. 'Co-optive power', Joseph Nye argued, 'is the ability of a country to structure a situation so that other countries develop preferences or define their interests in ways consistent with its own.'[31] This form of power derives from having a culture and ideology that are enticing, from being able to shape international norms to suit these, and from being able to structure international institutions, and, in turn, the consenting behaviour of other states. Not only did the United States enter the 1990s with far greater soft power than any other state, the highly interdependent and institutionalized nature of the world was increasingly privileging such power. In Nye's words, the 'United States retains more traditional hard power resources than any other country. It also has the soft ideological and institutional resources to preserve its lead in the new domains of transnational interdependence.'[32]

Anxiety

Each of the above celebrations admits, at the margins, mild anxiety about the potential aspects of the unfolding world order, whether it be fears that domestic isolationism would undermine the unipolar moment or that the historical world might intrude upon life beyond history. There were other strands in post-Cold War American thinking, however, in which anxiety was the predominant rather than the secondary impulse.

There were those who were deeply sceptical about the unipolar moment and its durability. Most vocal among these were the neorealists, who argued that the unipolar moment was precisely that, a 'moment'. A situation in which there is a single remaining superpower is one in which there is a profound imbalance of power, and history tells us that other states will do whatever they can to re-establish a balance. 'Other states, uneasy about America's dominant position, will equip themselves as Great Powers,' Kenneth Waltz wrote.[33] The United States could struggle to retain its pre-eminence, to use its current advantage to deter, co-opt or defeat potential challengers, but this was bound to fail. Even a policy of benign hegemony, marked by the provision of global public goods, would simply encourage other great powers to free ride, enhancing their own positions while draining the United States. More than this, a strategy of benign hegemony was either nonsense or it would be interpreted as such. An unbalanced hegemon was unlikely to be consistently benign, and attempts to export its values and prosecute its interests were more likely to be seen as threatening than comforting.[34] Unipolarity was thus destined to give way to multipolarity, and this would occur sooner rather than later. The problem was that this would make the world considerably more dangerous. John Mearsheimer argued provocatively that we were heading 'back to the future', returning to the multipolar instabilities that fuelled centuries of warfare in Europe. Bipolarity had been the key to global security, and once this had gone alliances would come unstuck, collective institutions, such as the

European Union, would erode, and national military and economic cooperation would intensify.[35]

This concern about a slide into multipolarity was re-inforced by a second group of commentators anxious about America's declining economic primacy. This concern pre-dated the end of the Cold War by at least a decade, but was given added impetus by America's grow-ing indebtedness and economic sluggishness in the late 1980s and early 1990s, and by the apparent dynamism of its principal rivals, particularly Japan. Contrary to those who attributed such decline to imperial overstretch, this group stressed the internal deficiencies of the American economy itself. The United States had not only become the world's largest debtor nation, its share of global pro-duction and trade had receded, and its level of industrial development had fallen behind Japan.[36] Reversing this trend became the catch-cry of those calling for a Demo-cratic presidency after 1992. The Reagan and first Bush Administrations were berated for neglecting the domestic roots of American power: '[O]n the morning after an ostensible American victory, the U.S. economy has fallen into a recession and our relative standing in the world has fallen in measures of economic growth, competitiveness, balance of trade, national debt, public health, and educa-tion,' wrote Harris Wofford, the newly elected Democrat Senator for Pennsylvania.[37] Decline of this sort was doubly problematic, as economic power was now con-sidered the currency of world politics. And, as John Zysman argued at the time, as 'economic power increases in import-ance, the basis for influence shifts from the domain of military force, where America remains strong, to the domain of economics, where its position is weakened.'[38]

The idea that the world was taking a multipolar turn, with all its attendant dangers, was given a special twist by Samuel Huntington. Like the neo-conservatives, he argued vigorously for the defence of American primacy, which Japan's 'strategy of economic warfare' was threatening.[39] His innovation, however, was to claim that '[g]lobal politics has become multipolar and multiciviliza-tional'.[40] The most distinctive thing about the post-Cold War era, he claimed, was the rise of identity politics, in which people seek answers to the question 'who are we?' by invoking their deepest of cultural values. At the broadest of levels, this was creating a world divided into civilizations. 'The most important groupings of states are no longer the three blocs of the Cold War but rather the world's seven or eight major civilizations.'[41] For Hunting-ton, relations between these civilizations would be much the same as relations between competing great powers – the struggle for power would be the norm, and conflict would be endemic. 'In this new world the most persuasive, important, and dangerous conflicts will not be between social classes, rich and poor, or other economically defined groups, but between peoples belonging to different cul-tural entities. . . . And the most dangerous of these conflicts are those along the fault lines between civilizations.'[42] The most dangerous of these fault lines, he argued, concerned 'the interaction of Western power and culture with the power and culture of non-Western civilizations', particu-larly those of the Islamic and Confucian worlds.[43]

These euphoric and anxious imaginings of the post-Cold War world did not exhaust debate within the United States, let alone beyond. There were some who anticipated a new multipolar order, but who saw it as desirable, as laying the foundations for a new concert of great powers and the equilibrium this might foster.[44] There were others who proffered their own visions of impending chaos that made Huntington's look mild by comparison.[45] The per-spectives surveyed above, however, were particularly prominent in America's struggle to comprehend the new world order and its emergent role. They also became ingredients, both major and minor, in the discourse of America's power that emerged ascendant almost a decade later.

The idealism of preponderance

One can read the 1990s as an interregnum, as a period in which Americans struggled to come to terms with life beyond the Cold War, and in which ever so gradually, through struggle and chance as much as rational adjustment, a rejuvenated neo-conservative ideology, or 'grand strategy', triumphed in Washington. Neorealists think that grand strategies are driven by the imperatives of the international system, that they are rational responses to external threats, constraints and opportunities. But the story of this ideological triumph is as much one of ideological inheritance and long-standing agendas as it is of sober strategic adjustment. The attacks of September 11 were certainly more than sufficient to catalyse such adjustment, but the die was cast well before then.

The neo-conservative ascendancy

Despite victory in the Gulf War, the presidency of George Bush senior was a disappointment to Reaganite neo-conservatives. America's capacity to set the agenda, provide decisive leadership in the UN Security Council and deliver devastating military force to uphold international law in far-flung parts of the world had been demonstrated, at least partially, by the first Gulf War. But the full potential of this capacity had never been realized. Not only was

Saddam Hussein still in power, constrained only by an ad hoc system of no-fly zones and economic sanctions, but Bush's vision of a new world order seemed increasingly vision-less, lacking both coherent purpose and effective punch. Bush's foreign policy credentials were never in question, having served both as ambassador to China and the UN, and as Director of the CIA. Yet his approach to the new world order was pragmatic and managerial, and he was criticized from all points of the political spectrum for offering 'foreign policy without strategy, management without leadership, a kind of competent drift'.[46] This was the context in which Krauthammer made his plea for the United States to seize the unipolar moment, a plea targeted at a Republican, not a Democratic, presidency.

It was unlikely that the neo-conservatives would gain much comfort from the Clinton Administration. In 1992, the American public was less animated about international affairs than it had been for more than a decade, and Bill Clinton was elected with a mandate to focus on a litany of persistent domestic troubles, from the parlous state of the economy to health care, education and urban crime. Slow to articulate his foreign policy agenda, Clinton's approach might best be described as a half-hearted Wilsonian inter-nationalism, the central motif of which was a commitment to the 'enlargement of democracy and free markets'. In the second of these areas the Administration scored some notable successes, such as the conclusion of the Uruguay Round of the General Agreement on Tariffs and Trade (GATT), the associated creation of the World Trade Organization (WTO) and the establishment of the North American Free Trade Association (NAFTA). Its record in promoting global democracy was less noteworthy, how-ever. Behind the rhetoric lay vacillation on conflict in the Balkans, an inconsistent pattern of dealing with human rights in authoritarian states and an ambivalent attitude towards the development of international law, most clearly apparent in the on-again-off-again approach to the International Criminal Court. This latter stance reflected a deeper ambivalence towards international institutions, in which declarations of support for multilateralism were contradicted by instances like the circumvention of the UN Security Council in the case of Kosovo. During its second term, the Administration's rhetoric and practice took a more unilateralist turn, partly in response to attacks from Congress.[47] Senior figures proclaimed repeatedly that the United States was the 'indispensable nation'. Echoing Louis XIV's claim that a king 'is of rank superior to all other men, he sees things more perfectly than they do',[48] Madeleine Albright argued that 'We stand tall and we see further than other countries into the future, and we see the dangers here to all of us.'[49] The neo-conservatives found little that was objectionable in Clinton's commitment to spreading democracy and promoting free trade, but they hated his weak and inconsistent internationalism, and his failure to give full expression to America's 'indispensable' role. Like Bush before him, Clinton had failed to capitalize on the unipolar moment; to articulate a clear and ambitious plan for the transformation of the global order according to American values, to lead forcefully and unilaterally if necessary, and to secure American primacy by bolstering its military predominance.

As the 1990s progressed, conservative forces challenged the Clinton Administration on multiple fronts. After the 1994 mid-term congressional elections, Newt Gingrich launched his 'Contract with America', setting out a conservative social and political agenda to rival the Administration's. This was a time of growing influence for the Christian Right, which came to have considerable sway over Republican policy. In the 1998 mid-terms, voter guides distributed by the Christian Coalition to millions of American homes claimed that on average Republican Representatives had voted according to the Coalition's agenda 88.7 per cent of the time, with Gingrich scoring 100 per cent.[50] The campaign against the Administration was not confined to its legislative agenda. Conservative groups inside and outside Congress scoured the Clintons' financial and personal histories, leading ultimately to the Lewinsky case, the Starr Commission and Clinton's near impeachment. In spite of this concerted campaign, Clinton left office after his second term with record popularity.

One of the less dramatic, though ultimately most influential, strands of the anti-Clinton campaign was waged by a group of neo-conservative specialists on foreign affairs. This group, which coalesced under the banner of the Project for the New American Century, included such figures as Jeb Bush, Dick Cheney, Donald Rumsfeld, Paul Wolfowitz, Richard Perle, Richard Armitage and Francis Fukuyama, most of whom would later gain senior positions in the administration of George W. Bush. Calling for a 'Reaganite policy of military strength and moral clarity', they sought a return to 'the essential elements of the Reagan Administration's success: a military that is strong and ready to meet both present and future challenges; a foreign policy that boldly and purposefully promotes American principles abroad; and national leadership that accepts the United States' global responsibilities'.[51] Donning the mantle of the Committee for the Present Danger, which had helped lay the ideological foundations for Reaganism, key members of the Project stressed a new 'present danger', a danger from within, the danger of American 'moral and strategic disarmament'.[52]

The Project for the New American Century proposed a grand strategy of unbounded ambition, encapsulated in an early article by Zalmay Khalilzad. Central to this strategy was the idea that the United States should 'seek to retain global leadership and to preclude the rise of a global rival or a return to multipolarity for the indefinite future',[53] an idea first articulated in 1992 in a memo leaked from Paul Wolfowitz's office in the Pentagon to the *New York Times*. Transforming the unipolar moment into a 'unipolar era', it was thought, would create an environment 'more open and more receptive to American values', more conducive to dealing with problems of nuclear proliferation, rogue states and low-level conflicts, and less prone to cold and hot wars among the great powers. To guarantee American primacy, and the realization of these goods, the United States had to prevent a hostile hegemon emerging in Europe, East Asia or the Persian Gulf, preserve American military pre-eminence, extend and strengthen the zone of peace among liberal democracies, and bolster the technological and productive bases of its economic strength.[54] In addition to these broad strategic goals, Project members insisted that the dangers posed by states such as Iraq and North Korea could only be met through 'regime change'.[55] They also stressed the need for the United States to counter threats from states with chemical, biological and possibly nuclear weapons by threatening nuclear retaliation, developing the capacity to pre-emptively destroy such weapons, and building active and passive defence systems.[56]

The Bush Doctrine

The triumph of these ideas was only partially due to their perceived merit in the marketplace of contending visions. To be sure, the Project for the New American Century was immensely successful in capturing the policy high ground within the Republican Party, particularly over the more cautious realists such as Henry Kissinger and Jeanne Kirk-patrick. Their broader victory, however, was due more to chance and circumstance than reason and persuasion. When the Supreme Court handed George W. Bush the 2000 presidential election, the Project's members moved from a position of minority protagonists in a vigorous public debate to one of policy mandarins. Even then, doubts over the legitimacy of Bush's election, and the fact that the Republicans quickly lost control of the Senate, partially stayed their hands. The attacks of September 11 changed all this. From that moment, the shackles were off. Convinced already of American power and righteousness, the spectre of an abiding yet amorphous global threat gave the Administration a mandate, in their view, to cement American primacy and unashamedly reshape the global order – unilaterally if necessary.

Before proceeding, a few words are needed about neo-conservative influence within the Bush Administration. The number of Project members who joined the Administration is striking, as is the similarity between their agenda and subsequent policy directions. But not all of Bush's cabinet came from this stable; Bush himself was never a member, and nor were Colin Powell or Condoleeza Rice. It is clear, however, that key Project members, particularly Donald Rumsfeld and Dick Cheney, have had considerable influence over the development of the Adminstration's grand strategy. Bush has injected a strong element of moral righteousness, Rice has been drawn ever closer to the hard-line centre of gravity, and Powell has fought rearguard actions to moderate the militant unilateralism of his Project colleagues. The net result is that the Administration's grand strategy has strong missionary overtones, and internal struggles have occurred over issues such as the need for Security Council endorsement. Yet, as we shall see below, it is the Project's neo-conservatives who have provided the basic template for Administration policy, even if that template has been modified by the politics of circumstance and implementation.

Central to the Administration's world view is a celebration of American predominance. The opening words of its 'National Security Strategy for the United States of America' reads: 'The United States possesses unprecedented – and unequaled – strength and influence in the world. Sustained by faith in the principles of liberty, and the value of a free society, this position comes with unparalleled responsibilities, obligations, and opportunity.'[57] In none of the Administration's public pronouncements or documents is this confidence even partially qualified. America's military and economic supremacy is understandably treated as a simple matter of fact. After almost a decade of sustained national economic growth and further improvements to military technology, the domestic foundations of American power are assumed secure. And with Japan in persistent recession, Europe grappling with sclerotic growth, Russia in visible decline, and China at best a handicapped competitor, potential challengers are thought to be well beyond the horizon. With such supremacy, it is taken for granted that Washington has the capacity to pursue and achieve a set of ambitious global objectives. 'We will work', the 'National Security Strategy' states, 'to translate this moment of influence into decades of peace, prosperity, and liberty.'[58] The Administration tips its hat to the need to cooperate with allies and touts its support for multilateral institutions, but this is always qualified by insistence that America 'will be prepared to act apart when our interests and responsibilities require'.[59]

In the early 1990s Nye and others sought to reaffirm American primacy by pointing to its unrivalled soft power. Even if other states were closing the material power gap, the United States had a culture and ideology of universal appeal. A decade later, fears about material decline have receded, but the idea that America is uniquely endowed with soft power has been thoroughly internalized. In fact, it is the supposed universality of American values, manifest in the culture and institutions of the American polity, that provides an unquestionable licence for the pursuit of Washington's global objectives. Echoing Fukuyama's thesis about the end of history, Bush's letter prefacing the 'National Security Strategy' declares that '[t]he great struggles of the twentieth century between liberty and totalitarianism ended with a decisive victory for the forces of freedom – and a single sustainable model for national success: freedom, democracy, and free enterprise'. Although the United States is considered both the embodiment of, and a beacon for, these values, they are said to be universally valid. 'These values of freedom are right and true for every person, in every society – and the duty of protecting these values against their enemies is the common calling of all freedom-loving people across the globe and across the ages.'[60]

When the memo proposing that the United States should seek to deter other great powers from challenging its primacy was leaked from Wolfowitz's office in 1992, the Administration of Bush senior went into damage control. Today it is declaratory policy. Confident of the material and ideological bases of American primacy, the Administration makes no bones about the fact that American 'forces will be strong enough to dissuade potential adversaries from pursuing a military build-up in the hopes of surpassing, or equaling, the power of the United States'.[61] This reflects both a belief that it is possible to achieve such a task – that the United States economy, ingenuity and industry can sustain perpetual military primacy – and a faith in the benevolent nature of American hegemony. Not only are American values those to which all rational peoples strive, but the United States provides, as would no other state, a long list of public goods essential for global order and well-being. In Robert Kagan's words, 'the truth is that the benevolent hegemony exercised by the United States is good for a vast portion of the world's population. It is certainly a better international arrangement than all realistic alternatives. To undermine it would cost many others around the world far more than it would cost Americans – and far sooner.'[62]

Securing American primacy in the service of American values is what the Bush Administration calls 'creating a balance of power that favors human freedom'.[63] After the Napoleonic Wars, Prince Metternich and other European leaders used the term 'balance of power' to describe a situation of equilibrium, in which states consciously adjusted their alliances to ensure that no single state could predominate. While Henry Kissinger and others hanker nostalgically for such a world, this is not the Administration's view. 'Balance of power' does not mean equilibrium; it means primacy, precisely the situation the European powers were seeking to avoid. It is sustained American ascendancy that will favour human freedom. Of course 'human freedom', like balance of power, has a distinctive meaning here – it means the freedom to choose the 'single sustainable model of national success: freedom, democracy, and free enterprise'. Those who are comfortable with the idea that we have reached the end of history, and that American values are indeed universal, will see this as natural and unproblematic. Others might be more troubled.

While the Administration is committed to deterring and defeating challenges to its hegemony from other rising great powers, it has sufficiently absorbed the democratic peace thesis to trust that conflict will be less likely if Russia and China can be encouraged to make successful democratic and capitalist transitions. The principal threats are thought to come from global terrorists and rogue states commanding weapons of mass destruction. The first of these is essentially new, exploding on to the agenda after the attacks of September 11. In the words of the 'National Security Strategy', the 'enemy is not a single political regime or religion or ideology. The enemy is terrorism – premeditated, politically motivated violence perpetrated against innocents.'[64] Confronting this enemy, the Administration has adopted a comprehensive offensive and defensive strategy, encompassing attacks on terrorist leadership; command, control, and communications, material resources, and finances; as well as strengthening 'homeland security'.

As we saw earlier, the Administration's concern with rogue states is not so new. Bush's infamous State of the Union reference to the 'axis of evil', comprising Iraq, Iran and North Korea, merely placed on the public agenda, in the most dramatic of fashions, one of the causes célèbres of the Project for the New American Century. The difference is that the case against these states, and in support of regime change, rests not just on their purported possession of weapons of mass destruction but on their alleged support for regional and global terrorist organizations. Hence Bush's speech on Iraq to the United Nations General Assembly sought to establish a tight connection between the two threats. '[O]ur greatest fear is that terrorists will find a shortcut to their mad ambitions when an outlaw regime supplies them with the technologies to kill on a massive scale. In one place – in one regime – we find all of these dangers, in their most lethal and aggressive forms, exactly the kind of aggressive threat the United Nations was born to confront.'[65]

While the Administration has repeatedly affirmed its commitment to international law and multilateralism, it appears that this is at best conditional. First, the

Administration has called for a revision to the laws of war to permit pre-emptive strikes in self-defence. 'The greater the threat, the greater the risk of inaction – and the more compelling the case for taking anticipatory action to defend ourselves, even if uncertainty remains as to the time and place of the enemy's attack.'[66] Since it is unlikely to gain the required two-thirds majority of the General Assembly to change the relevant articles of the Charter, it can only be assumed that it intends to change international norms through precedent-setting – yet law-breaking – acts of pre-emption, such as the war in Iraq and the extra-judicial execution of alleged al-Qaeda operatives in Yemen. Second, the concept of 'regime change' is a clear violation of the principles of sovereignty and non-intervention, for better or for worse. These norms were already being challenged in the 1990s in the name of humanitarian intervention, and the Administration is doing its best to portray regime change in Iraq or elsewhere, along with intervention in Bosnia or Kosovo, as all of a kind. Third, the Administration's attitude towards the collective security procedures of the United Nations Security Council appears to be that they are illegitimate and ineffectual unless they endorse Washington's prescriptions for international peace and security. As we shall see, the need to legitimate American actions has drawn it into these procedures, and once engaged its room to manoeuvre is circumscribed in critical ways. The fact remains, though, that the Administration struggles against the reality that these are deliberative fora, designed to produce negotiated rather than dictated decisions. Finally, the Administration has been willing to jettison international treaties when these constrain its strategic designs. For instance, claiming that the traditional logic of deterrence would not work against rogue states or terrorists, it withdrew from the Anti-Ballistic Missile Treaty with Russia so that it could construct a national missile defence system, appropriately nicknamed 'son of Star Wars'.

Conclusion

We like to think of national policies as rational constructions, formulated by pairing objective national interests with the most efficient of available means. Yet this is seldom the case. Policy-makers have ideological and normative commitments that define how they respond to new and old challenges. At times these are conscious; at times they are not. Polities have political cultures that frame debates about what constitutes national interests, making some goals and strategies seem natural and others literally unimaginable. History has structural features that produce patterns of continuity, some seen, and others not. History is also full of contingency, which throws up surprises. From the perspective of members of the Project for the New American Century, who were empowered in the Bush Administration, the Bush Doctrine would undoubtedly appear as a rational construction. But from a step or two removed, the victory of their ideas bears the marks of long-standing ideological commitments, dating back at least as far as the Reagan years; deep-rooted politico-cultural conceptions of American exceptionalism, democratic mission and security through world order tutelage; and the chance confluence of historical events.

I have described the resulting ideology of American power as 'the idealism of preponderance'. There is nothing idealistic about the fact of America's material preponderance, of course. Yet the idealistic aspects of the Administration's discourse about that preponderance should be clear to all. All ideologies have an idealistic dimension;

otherwise they would fail to command the imagination and inspire action. More than this, though, the Bush Doctrine is idealistic in other ways. To believe that overwhelming material power translates unproblematically into political influence and intended political outcomes is idealistic. To imagine that one's values are universal and that all reasoning human beings will see them as such is idealistic. And believing that one can pursue a project to transform the global system based on these values, without resistance, is idealistic. Each of these assumes that the United States stands outside or above the diversity of social and political life of the globe, or that this life has no autonomy. This, more than anything else, is idealistic, and it may ultimately prove self-defeating.

2

The Alchemy of Power

Buried within the 'idealism of preponderance' lies a theory of power. Not a theory in some deep social-scientific sense – with core assumptions, testable hypotheses and ambitions for law-like generalizations – but in the sense of a more or less refined set of assumptions that helps order the social and political universe of contemporary world politics, providing the touchstones or reference points for a particular form of American foreign policy. The neo-conservative writings introduced in the previous chapter advocate an American renaissance, a second century of American hegemony. They seek to awaken American policy-makers, and the American public one step removed, to the simple fact of American preponderance, to the historical opportunities such primacy provides and to the grave dangers of isolationism or misplaced multilateralism. A distinctive understanding of power informs this project, one that treats power as something actors 'possess', as something that flows unproblematically from unmatched material resources and ideological and cultural magnetism, and as something that is 'moral' when exercised in the pursuit of values one claims to be universal.

This chapter has two purposes. First, after a brief discussion of the concepts of power and hegemony, it draws out the principal dimensions of the neo-conservative theory of power. This theory, I shall argue, is deficient in three crucial respects: it assumes that material resources and ideological and cultural characteristics are necessarily 'empowering', that legitimacy can be self-ordained, and that cultural magnetism necessarily delivers political influence and compliance. Second, the chapter advances an alternative, 'social' conception of power and hegemony. My central claims here are that all political power is deeply embedded in webs of social exchange and mutual constitution; that stable political power – the sort that escapes the short-term vagaries of coercion and bribery to assume a structural, taken-for-granted form – ultimately rests on legitimacy; and that institutions play a crucial role in sustaining such power. All of this points to 'the paradox of hegemony', the fact that stabilizing power necessarily involves institutionalizing it, and this means creating social structures that have a degree of autonomy from the 'powerful' and that augment, at least partially, the agency of the 'weak'.

Two ideas of power

Power, as William Connolly observes, is an 'essentially contested concept', one that is value laden, internally complex and open to divergent interpretations.[1] No attempt is made here to resolve this contest, partly because it is beyond the scope of a small book, and partly because (by definition) 'essentially contested' concepts defy categorical definition. My goal is the more modest one of distinguishing between two broad conceptions of power, and making the case for one over the other, a case that I hope will be compelling even if it remains vulnerable to various lines of philosophical critique.

Barry Hindess usefully contrasts two conceptions of power: 'power as a simple capacity', and 'power as legitimate capacity'.[2] These may be treated as ideal forms, each exhibiting a number of distinctive characteristics that will enable us to locate both the neo-conservative theory of power and my own 'social' alternative. The first conception – power as simple capacity – resonates with much common usage. We invoke it when we speak of the physical power of the athlete to break a world record, or the intellectual power of the scientist to solve a problem in physics. We also invoke it when we refer to social or political power, but here we refer to the power of an actor to realize his or her goals by circumscribing, channelling, harnessing or transforming the preferences and actions of other actors.

This first idea of power has a number of features. To begin with, it is *possessive*. It imagines power as something that an actor owns, a tangible resource that he or she commands individually. We thus speak of the power of a president or a prime minister, or in international relations of the United States or Australia. Second, this view of power is *primarily material*. Guns and money are considered quintessential power resources, especially when it comes to relations between states. Hans Morgenthau, the great classical realist, lists geography, natural resources, industrial capacity, military preparedness and population as core elements of national power. Less tangible elements such as national character, national morale, quality of diplomacy, quality of government and ideology are also listed, but these are discussed as if they are akin to material resources, as if they too could be quantified and weighed in the scales of international power.[3] Third, the notion of power as simple capacity is *subjective*. That is, even so-called 'soft' aspects of power, such as ideology, values or beliefs, are seen as attributes of a single actor or subject;

they are not seen as having any intersubjective existence. Finally, and flowing from this last characteristic, this idea of power is *non-social*. Power is something that individual actors possess, and while the distribution of capabilities or balance of power between actors may be seen as a feature of a given social system, the processes, norms, institutions and structures of that society are not thought to be constitutive of power, at least not in any deep or meaningful sense.

The second idea of power – power as legitimate capacity – differs markedly from that outlined above. In general, it sees 'power as involving not only a capacity but also a *right* to act, with both capacity and right being seen to rest on the consent of those over whom power is exercised'.[4] This view of power is perhaps most famously expressed in Max Weber's idea that the state holds a 'monopoly of the legitimate use of physical force'.[5] Notions of 'right' and 'legitimacy' give this understanding of power several distinctive characteristics. First, it is *relational*, not possessive. Instead of power being something actors 'own' as atomistic individuals, it is something they gain only within relationships. Only when an actor seeks to have a transformative effect in relation to other actors can they be said to have, or not to have, power; and it is only in a relational context that the resources they conscript – material or otherwise – will have meaning or salience. Second, this view of power is *primarily ideational*. It holds that power is constituted not just by the distribution of material capabilities, but more fundamentally by social institutions, broadly construed as complexes of norms, rules, principles and decision-making procedures. Third, the idea of power as legitimate capacity is *intersubjective*. It not only attaches constitutive primacy to ideational factors, it denies that these can be treated as commodities possessed by particular actors. An ideology is powerless unless it is believed, and at this point it resides in the shared communicative realm between individual actors. Finally, as indicated in all of the above, this second view of power is inherently *social*. Social and political power is not simply dependent on the existence of more than one actor, it is a product of a society's defining practices and institutions.

These different views of power inform different understandings of hegemony. In the most general sense, hegemony describes the leadership of one state over others in an international system. This is usually taken to mean that the hegemonic state 'is powerful enough to maintain the essential rules governing interstate relations, and is willing to do so'.[6] However, this begs two questions. Is the exercise of power as a simple capacity a sufficient condition of hegemony or is something else required? And are rules to be understood as commands or types of social norms? The first view of power leads to the former understanding of hegemony, an understanding commonly identified with the claim by Athenian generals in Thucydides' *History of the Peloponnesian War* that 'the strong do what they have the power to do and the weak accept what they have to accept'.[7] The second view of power informs the latter conception of hegemony, in which hegemony is understood as a norm-defined, socially sanctioned status. This understanding is most commonly identified with the writings of Antonio Gramsci. In Robert Cox's words, a 'hegemonial structure of world order is one in which power takes a primarily consensual form, as distinguished from a non-hegemonic order in which there are manifestly rival powers and no power has been able to establish the legitimacy of its dominance'.[8]

These ideal conceptions of power and hegemony help orient what follows. Neither the neo-conservative theory of power nor my own alternative are simple expressions of these ideal types, but they are variations on these themes, and establishing reference points such as these is a useful way of illuminating what is consistent as well as distinctive.

The neo-conservative theory of power

As we saw in chapter 1, neo-conservatives call on Americans to embrace the reality of US power and to see it as a unique endowment with the potential to secure vital national interests, while furthering global peace, security and well-being. In her 2000 *Foreign Affairs* article, Condoleezza Rice criticized many Americans for being 'uncomfortable with the notions of power politics, great powers, and power balances'. Embodied in Clintonian foreign policy, this discomfort supposedly encouraged 'a reflexive appeal instead to notions of international law and norms, and the belief that the support of many states – or even better, of institutions like the United Nations – is essential to the legitimate exercise of power'. It also encouraged a naive neglect of the destabilizing potential of other great powers, which by 'reason of size, geographic position, economic potential, and military strength ... are capable of influencing American welfare for good or ill'. Americans had to wake up and recognize that 'Power matters, both the exercise of power by the United States and the ability of others to exercise it.' At the beginning of the twenty-first century, the United States finds itself 'in a remarkable position', with unrivalled power and 'on the right side of history'.[9]

One of the interesting things about the language of power is that, although it is 'essentially contested', politicians invoke it as though it has but one clear and unproblematic meaning. Yet Rice and her neo-conservative colleagues articulate a distinctive conception of power, one that approximates, despite some significant departures, to the first of our two ideal types.

To begin with, they present a classic statement of the idea of power as a possession, a commodity that the United States 'owns' as a unitary, atomistic actor. This was clearly apparent in Charles Krauthammer's early celebration of the 'unipolar moment'. 'American preeminence', he wrote, 'is based on the fact that it is the only country with the military, diplomatic, political, and economic *assets* to be a decisive player in any conflict in whatever part of the world it chooses to involve itself.'[10] A decade later, Stephen Brooks and William Wohlforth applauded Krauthammer's prescience, arguing that '[i]f today's American primacy does not constitute unipolarity, then nothing ever will'.[11] They claimed that '[n]o state in the modern history of international politics has come close to the military preeminence' of the United States; its economic dominance 'surpasses that of any great power in modern history', and it is 'the world's leading technological power'. In short, 'the United States has no rival in any critical dimension of power'.[12] This possessive view of power undergirds the Bush Administration's foreign and defence policies, with the opening line of its 'National Security Strategy of the United States' declaring that '[t]he United States *possesses* unprecedented – and unequaled – strength and influence in the world'.[13]

The idea of power as a possession is inherently quantitative; a nation's power is treated as a set of commodities or resources that can be counted and weighed against those possessed by others. This commodification of power leads to power being seen as 'primarily material', as non-material sources of power – such as values, culture or identity – are notoriously hard to quantify. We thus see neo-conservatives listing a standard catalogue of America's power resources, giving pride of place to military,

economic and technological pre-eminence. Guns
and money are seen as the bedrock of American power,
with technological supremacy serving as a turbo-charger
for both.[14] This stress on so-called 'hard' power resources, however, is not the only sense in which the
neo-conservative theory of power is primarily material.
Considerable weight is given to apparently 'soft' sources
of power, but these are discussed as if they were material
resources – commodities that could be counted and
weighed. As noted in chapter 1, neo-conservatives co-
opted the neoliberal argument that America's 'culture' is
a significant power resource, something that enables the
United States to pursue its global interests by winning the
hearts and minds of other peoples. Of particular interest
here is the stress placed on America's universal values,
particularly freedom, democracy and free enterprise.
These are understood as universal in two senses of the
word: in the sense of applying across all cultures and all
time; and in the sense of being comprehensible and desirable to all peoples. Yet, despite these dimensions of universality, these values are still seen as American
commodities that can be weighed against the cultural
commodities of other states. It is steadfastly assumed
that these values are American products – that they are
reproduced, interpreted and given meaning only through
American agency. Other polities and peoples are cast as
grateful receptors, not creative cultural agents.

The above features of the neo-conservative theory of
power point to its inherent 'subjectivity'. All self-narratives
are subjective, even if their success in constituting and pro-
jecting an actor's identity depends on them being clothed
in the mantle of objectivity. But the neo-conservative theory
of power is subjective in another sense as well. It is common
to speak of material power resources in subjective terms, as
attributes or possessions of a particular actor. As we shall

see on page 55, I am sceptical about this understanding. For the moment, however, I am concerned with the more controversial way in which neo-conservatives speak of non-material power resources in subjective terms. Freedom, democracy and free enterprise are presented as simultaneously universal and subjective; as transcendental and rational on the one hand, and American on the other. While this is a standard feature of all civilizational ideologies, it contradicts just about everything we know about the nature and function of social values. Even if it were true that these values originated in the United States and that Americans were primarily responsible for their global spread – propositions that Europeans and most post-colonial peoples would no doubt contest – the fact is that as soon as these ideas gain any social purchase beyond the American polity they must be regarded as intersubjective, not subjective. And to acknowledge their intersubjective nature is to recognize the agency of other polities and peoples in the articulation, reproduction and transformation of these values. Recognizing this, however, greatly complicates a theory of power, and makes it far less ideologically useful.

It will be clear by now that the neo-conservative theory of power is distinctly non-social. That is, American power is thought to exist independently of any constitutive international social forces, processes or institutions. Scholars advance different understandings of international society, but a common feature of all is the idea that through participation in such a society the basic interests and capacities of states can be transformed or redefined. It is strongest in recent constructivist writings on international society, which hold that states' identities, interests and powers are constituted by social rules and norms. But it is also found in both the pluralist and solidarist strands of the 'English School', as well as in neoliberal institutionalist writings. Robert Keohane, for example, acknowledges that the institutions of international society not only constrain activity, they 'prescribe behavioral roles'.[15] Nowhere in neo-conservative writings on American power do we find anything approximating this conception of international society. Krauthammer denied the existence of a society of states when he claimed that '[w]hat we have today is pseudo-multilateralism: a dominant great power acts essentially alone, but, embarrassed at the idea and still worshiping at the shrine of collective security, recruits a ship here, a brigade there, and blessings all around to give its unilateral actions a multilateral sheen'.[16] Rice adopted a similar position when she denied 'that the support of many states – or even better, of institutions like the United Nations – is essential to the legitimate exercise of power'.[17] In her view, it is the unity of America's national interests and objective universal values that guarantees such legitimacy, not the endorsement of an imagined community of states.

It is tempting to describe the above view of American power as realist, but this last point marks a significant departure from either classical or neorealist thought. Morgenthau's fifth principle of political realism states that:

Political realism refuses to identify the moral aspirations of a particular nation with the moral laws that govern the universe.... All nations are tempted – and few have been able to resist the temptation for long – to clothe their own aspirations and actions in the moral purposes of the universe. To know that nations are subject to the moral law is one thing, while to pretend to know with certainty what is good and evil in the relations among nations is quite another. There is a world of difference between the belief that all nations stand under the judgement of God, inscrutable to the human mind, and the blasphemous conviction that God is always on one's side and that what one wills oneself cannot fail to be willed by God also.[18]

The neo-conservative equation of America's national interests with those of humanity, and the subsequent assumption of their inherent legitimacy, not only violates this principle of political realism, but brings to the fore a crucial feature of their account of power: the fact that it is at once a theory of power and an ideology of power.

Achilles' three heels

In the late 1980s, Paul Kennedy advanced the provocative idea that great powers ultimately decline because of what they do to themselves, as a result of their dysfunctional power-maximizing strategies. For Kennedy, the problem was material: great powers, including the United States at that time, fall into an age-old trap of raising the costs of empire at moments of relative economic decline. In other words, the strategies they employ to boost their power actually serve to erode it.[19] Whatever the merits of Kennedy's argument – and it may well be too soon to tell – an analogous argument can be made today, but this time focusing on ideas. A central theme of this book is that the very theory of power currently prevailing in Washington is dysfunctional, partly because of its flawed assumptions, and partly because of its mismatch with the real world. I consider the latter in chapter 3. For now, I am concerned with three of its problematic assumptions, assumptions that through their very illogic, complacency and chauvinism encourage confident yet ultimately counter-productive power-maximizing strategies.

The first of these problematic assumptions is the neo-conservative understanding of the relationship between American power (understood as its material and material-like resources) and political influence. If the rhetoric is to be believed, the two exist in a relationship of simple causality – preponderance delivers influence. Evidence to support such claims is seldom provided; instead, rhetorical force is used to carry the argument. How could such overwhelming power resources not deliver systematic influence over political outcomes! Certainly this strategy has had its PR successes, evident in the repeated journalistic refrain that not since the days of Rome has there been a state as powerful as the United States. Yet the assumption that America's preponderance necessarily spawns political influence is belied by contemporary international politics. For a state with such unique endowments, the United States is experiencing a significant degree of diplomatic frustration. Across almost all issue areas, an Administration not shy of flexing its muscle is encountering a world with an annoying degree of autonomous opinion and dogged resistance. In reality, it seems, there is at best an attenuated relationship between raw power resources and control over outcomes. If this is true, then a theory of power that focuses solely on resources will help little in explaining these outcomes, and will provide a poor guide to national policy, as it neglects the other ingredients of influence.

The problem is nicely illustrated by the Brooks and Wohlforth article quoted on page 46. Most of the article is devoted to a celebration of American preponderance – 'the United States', we have heard, 'has no rival in any critical dimension of power'. This means that 'U.S. foreign policy today operates in the realm of choice rather than necessity to a greater degree than any other power in history'.[20] In the final pages of the article, however, there is a curious admission. Power, it turns out, does not automatically produce influence, and 'it is influence, not power, that is ultimately most valuable'.[21] The unmoderated, unilateral exercise of power may well erode American influence, as 'it is apt to reduce the pool of voluntary help from countries that the United States can draw on down the road, and thus in the end make life more difficult rather than less'. This would make it difficult to address 'the many issues – the environment, disease, migration, and the stability of the global economy, to name a few – that the United States cannot solve on its own'. The key to influence, Brooks and Wohlforth claim, is 'magnanimity', which the *Oxford English Dictionary* defines as 'generosity'. What they describe, however, is more akin to compromise, that is, to the mutual renegotiation of interests. The United States needs to demonstrate that it is 'interested in not just its own special interests but the interests of others as well'.[22] Power, it would seem, is only 'influential' when it is socially embedded. The problem is, of course, that the neo-conservative theory of power tells us – and American policy-makers – nothing about this social world.

The second problematic assumption is the neo-conservative view of legitimacy. At first blush, the problem appears simple indeed – the theory has no view of legitimacy. All that matters is the brute fact of American preponderance. On closer inspection, however, neo-conservatives do in fact articulate a concept of legitimacy, albeit a dangerously flawed one. The essence of their position is that American policies and practices are legitimate not because they are deemed so by the international community, but because American national interests are universal, because they serve the basic needs and aspirations of all the world's peoples. As indicated on page 49, Rice gave voice to this view in her 2000 *Foreign Affairs* article:

> The belief that the United States is exercising power legitimately only when it is doing so on behalf of someone or something else was deeply rooted in Wilsonian thought, and there are strong echoes of it in the Clinton

administration. To be sure, there is nothing wrong with doing something that benefits all humanity, but that is, in a sense, a second-order effect. America's pursuit of the national interest will create conditions that promote freedom, markets, and peace. Its pursuit of national interests after World War II led to a more prosperous and democratic world. This can happen again.... American values are universal.[23]

These ideas have been carried forward into the Bush Administration's policies and practices, evident most starkly in its Iraq campaign. Instead of support from the United Nations Security Council being the measure of the legitimacy of Washington's preferred strategy, the Administration tried to turn the tables, by making compliance with its strategy the test of the United Nations' legitimacy. The assumption is, of course, that America's strategy is already legitimate, based as it is on the universal nature of America's national interests.

The problems connected with this understanding of legitimacy are profound. First, as noted in the previous chapter, the view that American values and interests are universal and thus legitimate is distinctly idealist, a denial of the politics that inevitably surrounds the definition and mobilization of all values, even those of freedom, democracy and free enterprise. Second, and perhaps more seriously, the neo-conservative view of legitimacy borders on the delusional. No amount of asserting the self-ordained legitimacy of your policies and practices will make them so unless others believe it. Charles I and Louis XVI both suffered profound legitimation crises, yet, to the moment of their executions, they maintained their legitimacy in the eyes of God. Self-legitimation, even when alloyed to force, cannot replace or circumvent the actual social politics of legitimation. Finally, even if other states and peoples were to accept that American values and fundamental national interests – such as freedom, democracy and free enterprise – are universal, and also agree on the meaning and implications of these values, this does not mean that American policies and practices will be deemed legitimate. There is always an attenuated relationship between one's values, policies, strategies, tactics and practices, and humans have a remarkable capacity to see this attenuation and judge accordingly. The implication of these problems is that the conception of legitimacy contained within the neo-conservative theory of power can only blind American policy-makers to the actual and inevitable international politics of legitimacy.

The third problematic assumption integral to the neo-conservative theory of power is the supposed cultural magnetism of the United States. This magnetism is said to be one of America's principal power resources, with the global desire for American universities, films, fast food, music, clothes and, of course, values augmenting the country's already substantial political influence. In Josef Joffe's words:

> America's 'soft power'...looms even larger than its economic and military assets. U.S. culture, low-brow or high, radiates outward with an intensity last seen in the days of the Roman Empire – but with a novel twist. Rome's and Soviet Russia's cultural sway stopped exactly at their military borders. America's soft power, though, rules over an empire on which the sun never sets.[24]

We see here yet another expression of the assumed causal connection between power resources and political influence, this time applied to culture. If anything, however, the problems are multiplied. Let us assume that in one sense at least neo-conservatives are right, that many people around the globe do indeed covet certain 'American' (now globalized) cultural values and artefacts, from Ivy League education to Disneyland and Nikes. It is the height of blind chauvinism, however, to think that this necessarily translates into American political influence. To begin with, many of the world's citizens appear quite capable of holding at least two ideas in their heads at the same time. On the one hand, they might want to do a doctorate at Harvard, watch a Hollywood movie or wear Nike runners, but at the same time they can be deeply worried about the nature and consequences of American foreign policy. Second, even if it made sense to speak of culture as a power 'resource', it is a resource that defies control. Culture – in the form of values or artefacts – is inherently intersubjective, and, even if it does 'radiate outward' from a particular society, it is never passively received; it is always reinterpreted, grafted to other values and turned to new purposes. Both of these points are nicely illustrated by the example of the British Empire and Indian nationalists. In the late nineteenth and early twentieth centuries, young Indian elites flocked to Cambridge, Oxford and London universities. This did not mean, however, that they uncritically accepted imperial rule; on the contrary, they took the ideas of liberalism and democracy they imbibed in the imperial heartland and fashioned them into anti-imperialist nationalism.

A social conception of power

The above problems are integral to the neo-conservative theory of power; they stem directly from its political autism, its possessive, material, subjective and non-social character. I now wish to advance an alternative, social conception of power, one that is both heuristically more useful and practically less dysfunctional. The starting point for this conception is the proposition that a viable theory of power cannot focus solely on 'power resources', for, as Brooks and Wohlforth admit, these may relate only in the most attenuated way to patterns of political influence. When we describe a state as powerful, we are saying more than it has plenty of guns or money; we are saying that it can successfully realize its goals. To capture this, I propose defining power in a way that encompasses a modicum of control over outcomes. Here, I shall follow Weber in defining power as 'the probability that one actor within a social relationship will be in a position to carry out his own will despite resistance, regardless of the basis on which this probability exists'.[25] This is the definition I take Joseph Nye to be embracing when he describes power as 'the ability to effect the outcomes you want, and if necessary, to change the behavior of others to make this happen'.[26]

In referring to an 'actor within a social relationship', Weber's definition points to the inherently social nature of power. To grasp this nature, we must recognize that power is ubiquitous. In the first instance, it is a necessary characteristic of all social and political agency. To attribute agency to an actor is to suggest that they have some power to shape the social world around them, and no actor lacks agency (and hence power) altogether, even if it is merely a capacity for defiance or resistance.[27] Power is also ubiquitous in the sense that it is a prerequisite for all social goods and evils, for freedom and creativity as well as oppression and destruction. As Anthony Giddens observes, '[a]t the heart of both domination and power lies *the transformative capacity* of human action, the origin of all that is liberating and productive in social life as well as all that is repressive and destructive.'[28] The human agency that created the

Sistine Chapel was enabled by power as much as the bombing of Hiroshima and Nagasaki.

Power is not only ubiquitous; it is also inherently relational. Power is not something that atomistic actors own as a quantifiable commodity; it is something they gain only within social relationships. Power 'can develop only through *exchange* among actors involved in a given relation. To the extent that every relation between two parties presupposes exchange and reciprocal adaptation between them, power is indissolubly linked to negotiation: *it is a relation of exchange, therefore of negotiation,* in which at least two persons are involved.'[29] The lone individual, living outside of society but controlling abundant material resources, cannot be said to have power in any *politically* meaningful sense. It is only when an actor seeks to have a transformative effect in relation to other actors that they can be said to have, or not to have, power; and it is only in this relational context that the resources they conscript, material or otherwise, will have political or social meaning or salience. The United States tried to convince the United Nations Security Council that war was justified in order to disarm and depose the Iraqi leader, Saddam Hussein. Yet the extent of American power was determined only partly by the size of its military. America's moral authority, its capacity to make other members of the Security Council perceive the same level of threat, its ability to turn the issue into a test of UN authority, the vagaries of the inspection regime, the corralling effect of institutional processes and the behaviour of the Iraqis themselves were all significant forces in conditioning the power accessible to the United States.

There are some who argue that power ought to be distinguished from force. Power, on this view, is seen as the capacity to extract compliance from others, and while the threat of force might help induce such compliance, the exercise of force is evidence of non-compliance. 'Unlike power,' Robert Jackman contends, 'force does not induce compliance; the exercise of force is instead an admission that compliance cannot be induced by noncoercive means.'[30] For most students of international relations, this view is unlikely to convince, as it jars too readily with our deepest intuitions that when states use violence to achieve their ends they exercise, or at least seek to exercise, power. There is, however, an insight here that is worth retaining. When an actor resorts to force to direct the behaviour of others, it is apparent that they have lost or relinquished an important aspect of power: the ability to 'attract' voluntary compliance. The use of force to 'extract' compliance must thus be seen as a diminished or impoverished form of power, one that contrasts with more deeply socialized forms of power that conscript, in one form or another, the endorsement of other actors.

Rather than exclude force as a form of power, it is fruitful to imagine a continuum between ideal types of coercive and authoritative power. At the coercive end, force, or the threat of force, is an implement of power. At the authoritative end, legitimacy is. Coercive power is defined here as the infliction of pain or damage – or the withdrawal of something valued, such as patronage or affection – to compel another actor to behave in a particular way. Contrary to Jackman, this form of power is as relational as others. What constitutes effective coercion will depend on how the target actor understands its fundamental interests. An actor who is willing to die for a cause is not easily coerced by physical threats. A dictator is not easily coerced by threat of war if he or she believes that this will enhance personal prestige and galvanize national support. Authoritative power rests not on force but on legitimacy, defined here as the normative belief (well founded or otherwise) on the part of an actor that a command or rule *ought* to be obeyed. Consent based on a normative belief about the *rightness* of a directive or norm is thus the foundation of authoritative power.[31] While examples of these ideal types of power can be found in social life within, between and across states, most expressions of power are a mixture of these ideal types. A dictator may rule principally by coercive means, but he or she may also have a degree of personal charisma that induces a modicum of consent, however tenuous. The institutions of democracy might endure for centuries because of their legitimacy in the eyes of the citizenry, but this same legitimacy may license the use of coercion to suppress or compel a disenchanted or disenfranchised minority.

The use of coercion is often considered the 'real man's' form of power, the mark of a strong leader, strong state or well-disciplined international order. Yet the evidence suggests otherwise. Edmund Burke famously observed that 'the use of force is but *temporary*. It may subdue for a moment, but it does not remove the necessity of subduing again; and a nation is not governed, which is to be perpetually conquered.'[32] This quote points to several limitations of coercive power. First, relying on the use or threat of force, as well as that of bribery, leads to vulnerable, unstable rule – rule that depends on the vagaries of command, threat and sanction. Niccolò Machiavelli argued that it was better for a prince to be feared than loved, but ultimately he thought a glorious reputation was most important, and he counselled against the repeated use of coercion, as it fosters not fear but hatred, which guarantees opposition.[33] Second, coercive power is a costly source of rule. There are the simple yet substantial costs associated with the continued articulation of threats, monitoring of compliance and application of force, but there are also the hidden costs of foregoing the benefits of voluntary co-operation and assistance. Furthermore, because coercive power leads to unstable rule, it is difficult to predict and anticipate risks, and the costs associated with this tend to discourage corporations from investing in dictatorships. Third, coercive power is best suited to the realization of short- , not long-term interests. The Bush Administration decided to depose Saddam Hussein unilaterally, thus realizing its immediate aim. It is open to serious question, however, whether this disciplinary and exemplary use of force will, in the medium to longer term, increase the likelihood of democracy and peace in the Middle East, reduce threats from terrorism and weapons of mass destruction, enhance global peace and security, and facilitate the pursuit of America's litany of global interests. Finally, as all of the above indicates, coercive power might well deliver domination (rule by control), but not governance (rule by authority).

If the evidence points to coercive power's weaknesses, it also points to authoritative power's strengths. Although it must be cultivated not wielded, negotiated not inflicted, communicated not applied, authoritative power is ultimately essential to stable rule. Charles Merriam once wrote that power 'is strongest when it employs the instruments of substitution and counter attraction, of allurement, of participation rather than exclusion, of education rather than of annihilation'.[34] The reasons for this are threefold. First, authoritative power rests on sedimented beliefs about the legitimacy of governing agents, institutions and rules, and, while these beliefs require construction, communication and redefinition, their taken-for-granted quality, the fact that they often become naturalized, fosters stable rule. Second, authoritative power is less costly than coercive power. This is not to say that the cultivation of legitimacy is costless, only that it is boosted by the voluntarism of willing compliance and less encumbered by the costs of maintaining a comprehensive regime of threats and sanctions. Third, authoritative power is better suited to the realization of long-term interests than the use of force. As neoliberals have demonstrated, it is rational for a hegemon to socialize its power through participating in multilateral institutions if it seeks long- over short-term gains.[35] Finally, by definition, the cultivation, institutionalization and exercise of authoritative power fosters governance not domination.

For neo-conservatives, power and institutions are antithetical: material power is what matters, and institutions are no better than tinsel at a family Christmas party – they look pretty, but don't alter underlying social dynamics. Recall here Krauthammer's ridiculing of the United Nations: 'Except in a formal sense, it can hardly be said to exist.'[36] From the perspective of the social conception of power advanced here, however, power and institutions are inextricably entwined. Institutions are generally defined as sets of norms, rules and decision-making procedures that perform two functions: they shape actors' roles and identities, and they regulate their behaviour. Power is constituted by institutions in three crucial ways. To begin with, it is within the framework of institutions that power resources gain meaning. The most fundamental of these institutions are norms of friendship, rivalry and enmity. For friends, military resources are benign, even empowering. For enemies, they are threatening.[37] Second, societies ordain certain actors and actions with legitimacy, thus empowering them. But these acts of ordination are done either with reference to pre-existing institutional norms, such as the rules of the United Nations Charter, or through social processes of negotiating new norms. Either way, no actor or action can be defined as legitimate without reference to some institutional rule or norm, codified or otherwise. Institutions are 'legitimators' of power. Finally, institutions serve the vital function of regularizing power relations. In all social orders, both the strong and weak have an interest in making power relations stable and predictable. With notable exceptions, such as Mao Tse Tung's 'permanent revolution', few rulers want their power to be spasmodic, and few subjects want it to be erratic. Societies turn to institutions to regularize power relations because, by definition, rules and norms license or proscribe certain forms of agency or action *over time*. There is no such thing as an episodic rule or norm. For this reason, Giddens goes so far as to say that 'the most important aspects of [social] structure are rules and resources recursively involved in institutions'.[38]

In modern international society, three levels of institutions play a role in constituting power relations. At the most basic level, power is shaped by the deep 'constitutional' values of international society. The 'constitution of international society is a set of norms, mutually agreed upon by polities who are members of the society, that define the holders of authority and their prerogatives...'[39] The principle of sovereignty is the most famous of these norms, stipulating as it does that global power ought to be organized into centralized, territorially demarcated political units called states. Sovereignty has always existed in dialogue, however, with other constitutional values that define the types of polities that are entitled to sovereign recognition. And it takes on different meanings, and has different implications for the powers enjoyed by states, depending on whether norms of divine right or liberal democracy are ascendant.[40] Closer to the surface lies a second level of 'fundamental' institutions, the most prominent of which today are international law and multilateralism. These are the dominant practices that states employ to solve cooperation problems and facilitate coexistence, and they have an important impact on power relations by dictating how international rules should be legislated, interpreted and enforced. The United Nations stands at the intersection between these two institutions, and thus constitutes a crucial site for the definition and exercise of authoritative power. The final and most visible level of institutions is that of 'international regimes', which are practical expressions of international law and multilateralism in particular issue-areas. The Nuclear Non-Proliferation Treaty, the World Trade Organization, the Geneva Conventions, the Kyoto Protocol and the International Covenants on Human Rights are all examples of international regimes. This is the realm of substantive international rules, rules that define rights and obligations, lay down standards of behaviour, and specify decision-making procedures and modes of enforcement in distinct domains of international life. These rules can be empowering, in the sense of licensing certain forms of action, and constraining, in terms of delegitimating other forms.

'The paradox of hegemony'

It will be clear from what precedes that neo-conservatives are not interested in America being merely first among many – a great powers' great power, so to speak. Their goal is comprehensive hegemony, in which America's military might is so great as to make balancing pointless, and in which its 'universal' values inform the wholesale reform of the global political and economic order. Their view of hegemony, however, is curious to say the least. On the one hand, the possessiveness, materialism, subjectivity and asocial nature of their theory of power fits neatly with the idea that hegemony is simply the material capacity of a dominant state to dictate the rules of the international system. Or, as Krauthammer put it, 'unashamedly laying down the rules of world order and being prepared to enforce them'.[41] On the other hand, there is a perverted Gramscian strand to the neo-conservative view of American hegemony. American power is thought to rest in part on the magnetic attraction of its culture and the universality of its values, suggesting that it has a consensual basis. But, as we have seen, neo-conservatives have no notion of a social world beyond the United States, and without such a notion consent is reduced to nothing more than hungry reception. Because this view of hegemony is informed by the neo-conservative theory of power, we should not be surprised that it suffers from precisely the same problematic assumptions. It too rests on the beliefs that power resources unproblematically deliver political influence, that legitimacy is self-ordained and that cultural magnetism is so mesmerizing as to produce unreflective acquiescence to American foreign policy.

It is interesting to note here that the neoliberal alternative to this view of hegemony – articulated most prominently by Nye – suffers from similar problems. Unlike neo-conservatives, Nye does define power in terms of political influence, rather than just resources. Yet, for all of his talk about public-minded foreign policies and multilateral engagement, his view of American hegemony still fails to comprehend the politics of legitimacy, or to move far beyond the neo-conservative view of cultural magnetism. On the former, he would certainly not endorse the idea that America's foreign policy is legitimate simply because its national interests are universal. However, his view of legitimacy is not especially social either. American power would be deemed legitimate, he seems to believe, if the United States provides global public goods, defined as something that 'everyone can consume without diminishing its availability to others'.[42]

There is, however, no notion in Nye's writings that these goods would have to be negotiated internationally – they are treated as though they are objective and uncontroversial. One might ask, though, whether the maintenance of the balance of power, promotion of an open international economy, and maintenance of international rules and institutions – all of which he lists – fit this bill. Would it not be necessary to negotiate the nature of the balance of power, open economy and international institutions before their maintenance could become a source of secure legitimacy? On the question of cultural magnetism, Nye's position is not dissimilar to that of the neo-conservatives, who borrow much from his early book *Bound to Lead*. America's use of its soft power resources is a crucial source of political influence, enabling it to change others' preferences and hence their behaviour: 'If I can get you to *want* to do what I want, then I do not have to force you to do what you do *not* want to.'[43] Lost altogether here is any sense of the cultural agency or autonomy of the world's peoples, and Nye seems unaware of the ethical, and hence political, problems of seeking to change others' preferences to achieve America's ends.

The social conception of power elaborated in the previous section (pages 53–63) leads to a view of hegemony significantly different from those described above – a view that resists the temptations of self-ordained legitimacy and cultural chauvinism. Instead of seeing hegemony as a dominant state's brute capacity to 'lay down the rules', this view sees hegemony as a norm-defined, socially sanctioned status, and stresses the importance of legitimacy and consent in undergirding a leading state's power and influence. To quote Cox once more, 'to become hegemonic, a state would have to found and protect a world order which was universal in conception, i.e., not an order in which one state directly exploits others but an order in which most of the states (or at least those within reach of the hegemony) could find compatible with their interests.'[44] Three ideas are crucial here. To begin with, a hegemon must have substantial material power resources, but hegemony is ultimately a form of *social* hierarchy, based on status and recognition; it is not simply the pinnacle of a league table of raw material resources. Second, hegemony is an institutional type of world order, one in which generally recognized procedural and substantive norms cement social hierarchy, diminishing the need for coercion and exploitation. Third, hegemony is founded on the negotiation of identities and interests. For secondary states to find a world order compatible with their interests, the hegemon's leadership, as well as the procedural and substantive norms that frame such leadership, must bear the mark of those interests. Deaf and unresponsive great powers may realize domination, but they struggle to achieve hegemony. Finally, hegemons may use displays of force to impress their dominance, but force must be used sparingly and judiciously if it is not to undermine the social status and institutional bases of hegemony itself. If force is used in ways that are deemed illegitimate by the community of states, a gap emerges between the social identity of the dominant power and prevailing international norms, a gap that is ultimately corrosive of hegemony.

Bruce Cronin astutely observes that hegemony is characterized by a central paradox. 'Hegemons have the material capabilities to act unilaterally, yet they cannot remain hegemons if they do so at the expense of the system that they are trying to lead.'[45] The consent that other states grant a hegemon depends on it observing the institutional rules and practices of the hegemonic world order, and serious violations of those rules have the potential to erode that consent and, in turn, hegemony itself.

Hegemons thus have a strong incentive to avoid socially corrosive unilateral actions, yet domestic politics can drive them the other way. In Cronin's words, 'hegemons possess the capabilities and will to act unilaterally in pursuing their own interests. This raises expectations among domestic political actors and state officials that the government will pursue its own course when its interests are at stake.'[46] To sustain the consent of other states, hegemons must resist the pull of domestic politics and do two things. First, and this is the point emphasized by Cronin, they must maintain the basic procedural norms of the system, which means recognizing the legal equality of all states, observing the rules like others, permitting their responsibilities to delimit their freedom and accommodating secondary powers.[47] Second, they must recognize that new procedural and substantive norms must be negotiated, not dictated. This is partly because norms are not commands; they are socially sanctioned standards of behaviour. But it is also because other states require recognition as social agents with identities and interests worthy of respect, a point made by no less a neo-conservative than Francis Fukuyama.[48]

Conclusion

Neo-conservatives often claim that the United States is a status quo power, and thus its hegemony is benign. It is other great powers, such as China and perhaps Russia, that are revisionist, and rogue states even more so. Chapter 1 sought to show the fallacy of this claim, by describing how neo-conservatives within the Bush Administration have embarked on an idealistic quest for renewed American hegemony, the unilateralism and ambition of which is deeply revisionist. This chapter has taken the discussion one step further. I have sought to distil the neo-conservative theory of power that informs the Bush Administration's grand strategy and to identify its principal weaknesses, namely, its flawed understandings of the relationship between material power and political influence, the nature of legitimacy, and the politics of cultural interaction and exchange. I then outlined an alternative social conception of power, one that deals more adequately with each of these issues. This conception, I suggested, exposes the central paradox of hegemony: that stable, enduring leadership requires power to be socially embedded, and that unilateral action is socially corrosive, with implications both for the hegemon and world order.

Current discussions of American power tend to focus narrowly on the quantification of power resources, and not surprisingly conclude that the United States has unrivalled preponderance. This not only misses the important social bases of power highlighted in this chapter, but also the importance of context for the exercise of American power. America's political influence is determined not only by its attributes at a particular time – material, social or otherwise – but also by the environment in which it seeks to define its identity and formulate and pursue its interests. Not all international systems are the same; they have varied notions of legitimate statehood, varied institutional profiles, varied relationships to wider social forces, etc. Some systems are amenable to Procrustean power projection strategies, while others demand more subtle practices. The following chapter moves the discussion from the abstract to the concrete, exploring the differences between the world immediately after 1945, when the United States last enjoyed a form of hegemonic leadership, and the world today, which poses fundamental challenges for a project of hegemonic renewal.

3

The Real World

We often say that a particular 'idea's time has come', by which we mean that it fills a void, meets a pressing need, articulates with immanent social processes or resonates with other ascendant ideas, values or beliefs. The concept of sovereignty was an idea whose time had come by the middle of the seventeenth century, as had the idea of a Concert of Europe after the Napoleonic Wars and the Congress of Vienna. Keynesian economics' time came after the Great Depression, and, in the wake of two world wars, Europe was ready for ideas of regional integration. Sadly, the same cannot be said for the neo-conservative view of power and hegemony that informs the Bush Doctrine. Not only is it internally flawed – as the previous chapter demonstrated – it is also incompatible with the basic structures and processes of contemporary world politics. It is, in this sense, not unlike French strategic culture prior to the Second World War – dangerously at odds with reality.[1]

Of course, hardliners within the Bush Administration would disagree categorically. For them, the world today is akin to the immediate post-1945 world. Then, as now, America was materially pre-eminent, the world faced grave threats and challenges, and the unwavering exercise of American power created a more peaceful and prosperous world order, one that served America's interests as well as humanity's. Drawing such an analogy between a past golden age and the world of today is rhetorically powerful, but is also bad history and even worse contemporary analysis. It assumes that just because America was materially preponderant after the Second World War, and that it finds itself in such a position again today, it follows that the two historical moments are analogous. The fact is, though, that the two eras in which America has been materially predominant are radically different, with significant implications for American influence abroad.

This chapter explores the disjuncture between the neo-conservative understanding of power and contemporary world politics. It begins with a brief exposition of the over-romanticized post-1945 analogy, including the way in which it has been invoked to justify everything from global tutelage to the invasion of Iraq. I then embark on a systematic, although by no means exhaustive, comparison of the world today with that of half a century ago. The comparison focuses on five points of structural difference: the level of security dependence among the great powers, the nature of international economic association, the density of institutionalization, the relative autonomy of the society of states and the diffusion of normative agency. In each of these areas, the two worlds stand apart, and it will be fundamentally more difficult to establish and sustain hegemonic power in today's world than it was immediately after the Second World War. This difficulty is greatly compounded by the global consolidation of two phenomena: the system of sovereign states, and the liberal market economy. These processes have had a number of serious side-effects, including the 'domestication' of war, the persistent maldistribution of global wealth and the crisis in the global ecosystem, each of which poses a fundamental challenge for American leadership and effective global governance.

'Remembrance of things past'

The use and abuse of history is one of the most seductive and powerful rhetorical techniques available to politicians pursuing grand national projects. Ernest Renan once wrote that to 'have common glories in the past, a common will in the present; to have done great things together, to will to do the like again – such are the essential conditions for making a people'.[2] Narratives of nationhood are thus narratives of history, and they invariably involve the celebration of events and achievements that 'made us who we are', as well as the systematic forgetting of less edifying facts that 'were in the past, and for which we cannot be held responsible'. The celebration of constitutive moments in a nation's history is, however, seldom an act of faithful or nuanced representation or interpretation. Moments are selected to suit the contemporary political needs of the narrator, and their nature and meaning is crafted to give them a certain symbolic resonance. This is particularly apparent in the rhetorical use of historical analogies. Political elites invoke select moments in the past to license their preferred policies and strategies – 'we did this in the past and it made us great, so we should do it again' – and to discredit others – 'fools did this before and they paid heavily, so we should not repeat their mistakes'. The political use of analogies is, however, inevitably a project of simplification and reification; it is about raising to the fore a supposed point of commonality while simultaneously obscuring all points of difference.

Since the neo-conservative project is one of hegemonic renewal, it is not surprising that it is justified with reference to a perceived golden age of American power, the period following the Second World War. The repeated

theme here is that fifty years ago the United States stood at
the pinnacle of world power, and yet, unlike great powers
before it, strove not for domination but benevolent hegemony. In Robert Kagan's words:

> There was a time when the world clearly saw how different
> the American superpower was from all the previous aspir-
> ing hegemons. The difference lay in the exercise of power.
> The strength acquired by the United States in the after-
> math of World War II was far greater than any single nation
> had ever possessed.... That the American people 'might
> have set the crown of world empire on their brows,' as one
> British statesman put it in 1951, but chose not to was a
> decision of singular importance in world history and rec-
> ognized as such.[3]

This theme of benevolent hegemony is complemented by
that of dutiful heroism. Fighting the wars against terrorism
and rogue states is certainly justified with reference to self-
interest – to the need and right to combat imminent
threats to America's national security – but they are also
justified with reference to America's tradition of combating tyranny, with force if necessary. In his 2003 State of the
Union Address, President Bush said:

> This threat is new; America's duty is familiar. Throughout
> the 20th century, small groups of men seized control of
> great nations, built armies and arsenals, and set out to
> dominate the weak and intimidate the world. In each
> case, their ambitions of cruelty and murder had no limit.
> In each case, the ambitions of Hitlerism, militarism, and
> communism were defeated by the free peoples, by the
> strength of great alliances, and by the might of the United
> States of America.[4]

All of this is a prelude to the main message – that America
once again enjoys an unparalleled margin of power, that

the world faces grave challenges and that the United States has the opportunity, even responsibility, to don the mantle of global leadership. As Bush declared, 'Once again, this nation and our friends are all that stand between a world at peace, and a world of chaos and constant alarm. Once again, we are called upon to defend the safety of our people, and the hopes of mankind. And we accept this responsibility.'[5]

This invocation of a prior golden age has been used to justify not only the broad sweep of the Administration's grand strategy, but also to specific policy initiatives, none more so than the campaign to disarm and dethrone Saddam Hussein. Here the rhetoric has two components. The first involves the spectre of Munich, an event that has long epitomized the dangers of appeasing duplicitous dictators. In Kagan's words,

> Wilson's 'war to end all wars' was followed a decade later by an American secretary of state putting his signature to a treaty outlawing war. FDR in the 1930s put his faith in non-aggression pacts and asked merely that Hitler promise not to attack a list of countries Roosevelt presented to him. But then came Munich and Pearl Harbor, and then, after a fleeting moment of renewed idealism, the plunge into the Cold War.[6]

The second component involves drawing an analogy between Iraq and Japan and Germany. One of the Administration's principal justifications for war on Iraq was that it would produce a flower of democracy in the Middle East and that it would transform the political face of the region, facilitating even the resolution of the Israeli–Palestinian conflict. In response, critics have highlighted Washington's less than accomplished record of creating democracies out of war. The models, the Administration claims, are Japan and Germany. In justifying war with Iraq, President Bush told the American people that: 'After defeating enemies, we did not leave behind occupying armies; we left behind constitutions and parliaments.'[7] This analogy has little impressed experts on either Japan or Germany. Chalmers Johnson, the renowned Japan specialist, wrote that the 'plan won't work for the simple reason that Iraq is not Japan. The Bush White House and the Rumsfeld Pentagon seem to know next to nothing about Japan.... I doubt that a group of heavily armed American infidels can bring "democracy" to Iraq, but I know for certain that what happened 50 years ago in Japan is no model.'[8]

Because the Bush Administration's grand strategy is revisionist – seeking as it does to reassert American hegemony within a transformed global order – its political rhetoric not only harks back to a golden age, but also draws a sharp contrast with the immediate past, pre-September 11. There has been much debate about whether September 11 was 'the day the world changed', the moment when the familiar dynamics and parameters of world politics shifted for ever.[9] This debate has not, however, had much airing within the Administration – clean breaks with the past are too useful as justifications for bold new agendas. Of course, the Administration's understanding of this recent turning point is conditioned by the realist dimensions of its world view. From this perspective, what changed was the nature of threats and challenges to American security and power. Secretary of Defense Donald Rumsfeld's 2002 Report to Congress states: 'The events of September 11 presented a different view of the world: The 21st century security environment is different from that we faced in the 20th century – in important ways it is more complex and dangerous.'[10] This sense of a fundamental security disjuncture has licensed wholesale changes to America's military-strategic doctrine and posture. The new 'forward-leaning' policy focuses on the capabilities of other actors not threats, prioritizes offensive compellence strategies over deterrence, seeks to expand the right of self-defence to include preventive war, privileges ad hoc 'coalitions of the willing' over established alliances, and attempts to blur the operational distinction between nuclear and conventional warfare.[11]

Worlds apart

The neo-conservative use of history provides many openings for critique. My concern here, however, is with their master analogy, the proposition that we now stand at a moment in history akin to the post-1945 golden era of American power. As we saw above, this analogy is based on two claims: first, that at both moments America has stood at the pinnacle of world power (understood in terms of a preponderance of material power resources); and second, that at both points in history the world faced grave challenges. Nothing that follows contests either of these assumptions, although I differ on the nature of the challenges. It seems incontestable that the United States once again enjoys a significant preponderance of power resources, particularly of a material kind, and few would wish to deny the multiple difficulties that global society now faces. My line of critique is thus somewhat different. The neo-conservatives' master analogy is viable only if we restrict our gaze to the league table of national power resources, in which case the two periods have much in common. But if we broaden our gaze to survey the wider contexts in which America has enjoyed material preponderance, then the two periods appear radically different. It is this contextual difference, along with the internal flaws in the neo-conservative theory of power, and the dysfunctional policies this engenders, that ultimately frustrates the translation of America's power resources into effective political influence.

My comparison of the two worlds focuses on five axes of difference: the level of security dependence among the great powers; the nature of international economic association; the level of institutionalization; the relative autonomy of the society of states; and the diffusion of normative agency. These axes do not exhaust the differences between the two worlds, but they are significant in two respects. First, they are all axes of *structural* difference, features of international and world society, not properties of individual states. They thus stand as social constraints and incentives, conditioning and channelling the behaviour of even the most powerful actors. Second, together they are reasonably comprehensive. They encompass features of international life emphasized by a wide cross-section of scholars, from realists and neoliberals, to international society theorists and constructivists. My understanding of these features may differ from the standard interpretations given by these scholars, but I trust that they will nonetheless recognize the centrality of these aspects of international life.

Security dependence

One of the principal contextual differences between the immediate post-1945 period and today concerns the degree of security dependence and common threat perception among the great powers. As we have seen, neo-conservatives argue that the two periods are analogous because the United States has enjoyed a significant margin of material preponderance in both, particularly military preponderance. The assumption here, as chapter 2 explained, is that such preponderance will unproblematically deliver political influence, just as it did fifty years ago. This ignores, however, the crucial role that security dependence and common threat perception among the great powers played in sustaining America's post-1945 influence, as well as the far lower levels of such dependence and threat perception today.

In the post-1945 period, the non-communist sphere of the international system was characterized not just by America's military primacy, but by the exceptional nature of the United States' military position. Of the major Western states, the United States was the only one with a viable capacity to defend itself and its friends. Britain and France were militarily exhausted, and Germany and Japan were disarmed. As the Cold War escalated, these states became fundamentally dependent on the United States for their existential security, a dependence reinforced by their strong sense of a common threat. This is not to suggest that the United States was always confident of its exceptional position. The need to compete with the Soviet Union loomed large, and for much of the 1940s and 1950s Washington feared that local communists would gain the upper hand in a number of European countries. Furthermore, America and its allies did not always agree on the precise nature of the communist threat, and their perceptions evolved and diverged as the Cold War evolved. It should also be noted that the junior allies' level of security dependence was nowhere near as profound in the 1980s as it had been three decades earlier. My point is simply that at the peak of American post-war hegemony – when the United States was busily 'laying down the rules' of the new world order – Washington had the other non-communist powers deeply dependent upon its protection, a dependence that was bolstered by a robust sense of common threat. This situation, as much as the magnitude of America's military advantage, was unique in modern international history.

The situation today is markedly different. The United States enjoys military primacy, but its position is not exceptional. To be sure, it has the only military with global reach, its forces are quantitatively and technologically leagues ahead of the rest, and its military budget dwarfs that of its nearest contenders, even when combined. Yet the other major powers are no longer deeply dependent on the United States for their existential security, and they share at best only a thin sense of common threat. The five permanent members of the United Nations Security Council all have durable second-strike nuclear arsenals, and Japan and Germany have respectable, technologically advanced self-defence forces, capable of meeting most threats short of unlikely invasions by Russia or China. Both Moscow and Beijing have at best precarious security relationships with the United States, and while America's traditional allies are committed to the United States remaining engaged in their regions, disagreements frequently emerge with Washington over the nature and extent of that engagement. The general lack of existential security dependence on the United States is in part a product of, and compounded by, the lack of a strong or coherent common threat perception among the major powers, or even a significant group of them. Since September 11, Washington has done its best to present the nexus between global terrorism and rogue states as a general threat to the community of states, but since the overthrow of the Taliban in Afghanistan the 'coalition against terrorism' survives primarily as a global network of policing and intelligence cooperation, and the Bush Administration has only managed to attract opposition to its new doctrine of preventive war with its first application in Iraq.

Economic association

As noted in chapter 1, many scholars in the late 1980s were concerned with America's relative decline, not its further ascendance. Reaganism had pushed the United States into the classic trap of imperial overstretch, raising the costs of hegemony at a time of relative economic decline. If anything, therefore, a contrast was drawn with the immediate post-1945 period, not an analogy. By the end of the 1990s, however, the situation was reversed. The longest period of sustained economic growth in American history had pushed the United States' share of global GNP from around 23 per cent to 33 per cent. This dramatic resurgence did much to encourage the neo-conservative project of hegemonic renaissance, and provides one aspect of the analogy they draw between the immediate post-war period and today. The problem is, of course, that this analogy obscures crucial contextual differences between the two periods, and again these have a significant bearing on Washington's ability to translate its material resources into political influence. The most important of these differences concern the relative economic dependence of the great powers and the scope for institutional entrepreneurship.

As in the military realm, after the Second World War the United States' economic position was not only pre-eminent, it was exceptional. This was starkly apparent in the sheer size of the American economy, which in 1953 still accounted for nearly 45 per cent of global GNP. More than this, though, the strength of America's position was evident in two other features of the post-war system. First, for at least a decade after the Second World War, Western European states and Japan were as dependent economically on the United States as they were militarily. By 1948 Europe's post-war recovery had stalled, and, fearing that prolonged recession would encourage the spread of communism and undermine the American economy, the United States instituted the five-year Marshall Plan that injected $13.3 billion into Western European economies. This degree of dependence soon dissipated, and, as the Cold War escalated, Washington feared that competition with the Soviets might undermine the US economy. The fact remains, though, that at the time when the United States was shaping the contours of the post-1945 international order, the major non-communist powers were economic dependants. Second, after 1945, the United States was able to pursue its international economic interests as a rule-entrepreneur in an underdeveloped institutional environment. This is not to say that the rules of the Bretton Woods institutions were little more than dictates from Washington – far from it. Rather, it is to suggest that the United States was able to assume leadership in the creation *de nouveau* of a complex system of international economic institutions. Never had a state enjoyed such an opportunity in the past, and never has one since.

At the beginning of the twenty-first century, few of these enabling conditions remain. It would be absurd to suggest that a 33 per cent share of global GNP contributes little to American power and influence. Yet, although the size of the American economy gives Washington certain structural advantages – such as the leverage that comes with denying, or threatening to deny, market access – these advantages are not what they once were. To begin with, the United States encounters the other major powers (with the possible exception of Russia) as substantial economies, not as economic dependants. Economic interdependence is the order of the day, and, while the United States may be less sensitive and vulnerable than many other states to developments that occur elsewhere in the global economic web, it has an enormous amount invested in the health of the world economy, just as other powers have much riding on the health of the American economy. Furthermore, the United States no longer enjoys the creative freedom of a rule-entrepreneur in an emerging institutional order. The world economy is now densely institutionalized, so that although the United States has institutional advantages, such as weighted voting rights in the World Bank and the International Monetary Fund (IMF), it is also subject to a web of reciprocally binding rules, most notably those governing international trade. In such a world, as the following section explains, institutional innovation takes place within a pre-structured institutional environment, in which the creative strategies of actors who do not wish to exit are delimited by existing procedural and substantive rules.

Institutionalization

Unlike military and economic primacy, institutionalization does not feature in the neo-conservatives' master analogy. As chapter 2 explained, their view of power is atomistic and subjective, and thus institutions do not rate as sources of American power, either in the immediate post-1945 period or today. It is crucial, however, that we consider variations in institutionalization, as all but the most die-hard realists agree that the nature and density of international institutions affects the exercise and expression of state power, even if not all would subscribe to the constructivist version of this argument elaborated in chapter 2.

There is a standard narrative about American institutional innovation after the Second World War. The United States, at the pinnacle of world power, saw that it was in its long-term interests to sponsor the construction of an ambitious institutional architecture to foster international peace, economic growth and humanitarian well-being. More than this, it was prepared to pay the substantial costs of international collective action to achieve this goal. At one level, this narrative is broadly correct: the United States did devote considerable energies to the construction of post-war institutions. At another level, however, it is misleading. Washington embarked on its programme of institutional construction within a pre-existing institutional environment. Not in the sense that a wide network of functional regimes survived the war, although some certainly did, but in the sense that the basic norms of multilateralism and international law that informed Washington's constructions were enshrined almost a century earlier. What the United States did was give concrete institutional expression to these principles in a broad array of new regimes. Prominent among these were the Bretton Woods economic institutions mentioned in the previous section, but they also included the United Nations itself, the major human rights instruments and, over time, the principal arms control agreements. The real story of American post-1945 institutional innovation is thus one of normatively pre-structured design, and relatively unfettered mass construction.[12]

The situation today differs in three crucial respects. First, as in the post-1945 period, the current institutional environment is normatively pre-structured. That is, states that wish to create new frameworks of cooperation encounter a set of entrenched norms of practice that favour certain types of institutional cooperation over others, the most prominent of which remains the norm of multilateralism. The principal difference between now and the earlier period is that this norm has become routinized through the construction and functioning of thousands of multilateral regimes, operating in all issue-areas. States frequently engage in other institutional practices, such as bilateralism, but the norm is that multilateral institutions will provide the background framework of cooperation in all of the most crucial areas, most notably in the security and economic realms. Second, to a far greater extent than in the post-war period, the scope for institutional change or revision is procedurally pre-structured. At the most general level, multilateral norms not only prescribe the types of institutions states should establish, but also the mechanisms through which changes to existing rules should be made. At a more specific level, particular institutions have their own procedural rules about revision. When the Australian government says that it would like to see the United Nations Charter changed to allow greater latitude for pre-emptive war, this can only be done by obtaining the requisite two-thirds majority of the General Assembly. Third, the density of institutionalization is far greater today than ever before. Virtually all aspects of international cooperation are now institutionalized, creating a complex web of procedural and substantive rules. This greatly complicates institutional politics, simultaneously empowering states, by giving them opportunities to 'institution-hop' to better realize their interests (as Western powers did in the Kosovo crisis, hopping from the Security Council to NATO), and constraining them, by exposing states that fail to abide by the rules in one area to punishment in another.

Relative autonomy of the society of states

International relations scholars frequently draw two important distinctions. The first is between an 'international system' and 'an international society'. The former 'is formed when two or more states have sufficient contact between them, and have sufficient impact on one another's decisions, to cause them to behave – at least to some measure – as parts of a whole'.[13] The latter, in contrast, 'exists when a group of states, conscious of certain common interests and common values, form a society in the sense that they conceive themselves to be bound by a common set of rules in their relations with one another, and share in the working of common institutions'.[14] The second distinction is between international society and 'world society', the latter involving not only 'a degree of interaction linking all parts of the human community to one another, but a sense of common interest and common values, on the basis of which common rules and institutions may be built'.[15]

The neo-conservative master analogy rests on a systemic understanding of international relations, in which the material preponderance of America, both fifty years ago and today, is what matters, rather than the changing politics of an amorphous international society or world society. We have seen on page 81, however, that institutions are an enduring feature of international life, that the United States has in the past played an important role in constructing the present institutional architecture, and that over the last fifty years this architecture has become more complex in crucial ways. We have not yet considered, though, another significant aspect of global social change since 1945 – the changing relationship between international society and world society.

Because states are social constructs – products of deeper social forces – international society has never been truly autonomous from world society. Prior to the Napoleonic Wars, state sovereignty rested on the doctrine of the divine right of kings, but this doctrine was not just a feature of absolutist international society, it was a cultural attribute of European society in general. We can, however, speak of variations in the relative autonomy of the society of states.

The fact is that in the heyday of American hegemony international society was not as permeated by the actors and processes of world society as it is today. There are celebrated examples of non-state actors affecting the principles and practices of international society prior to and within this period, most notably the anti-slavery movement, the role of non-state actors in codifying the laws of war, and the agenda-setting contribution that such groups made to the promulgation of the major human rights instruments. It remains the case, though, that 'old diplomacy' dominated international relations until the Second World War, and in its wake states generally succeeded in quarantining international institutional politics from the forces of world society.

At the beginning of the twenty-first century, international society has become increasingly embedded in world society. In areas as diverse as arms control, environmental protection, international criminal law, global financial regulation, WTO negotiations, and even the controversy surrounding war in Iraq, state to state negotiations have been enveloped in, and conditioned by, the politics of non-state actors, from 'moral entrepreneurs', such as Amnesty International and Greenpeace, to transnational business groups. This trend has been encouraged by three factors. First, because a liberal international order rests on the twin pillars of democratic sovereignty and international free trade, its core norms simultaneously provide a rationale for the modern state and empower non-state actors that invoke those norms to delimit or channel state power. As in domestic society, liberalism is both constitutive and corrosive of state authority. Second, non-state agency in world politics has been greatly facilitated by the communications and technological revolutions associated with the amorphous processes of 'globalization'. It is now common for state representatives in international fora to lament (or admire) the organizational adroitness of non-state actors, and their mastery of global telecommunications has contributed substantially to the phenomenon of global protest, evident most dramatically in anti-globalization rallies in Seattle and elsewhere, as well as the global day of protest against the war with Iraq on 15 February 2003. Third, the 'doorman' role played by international organizations has been a crucial factor in augmenting the non-state forces of world society. Although these organizations are created 'by states for states', they often evolve a degree of autonomy, and, as they redefine their mandates, they frequently open the door to civil-society actors.[16]

While neo-conservatives understand international relations in systemic terms, bracketing international and global social forces from their world view, they have become increasingly uneasy, almost to the point of hysteria, about the growing political salience of non-state actors. Evidence of this is the recent conference held by the conservative think tank, the American Enterprise Institute. Speakers attacked non-governmental organizations (NGOs) for pursuing a left-liberal agenda of global governance in alliance with multilateral organizations such as the United Nations, an agenda that sought to constrain states and corporations. In an attempt to fight fire with fire, the Institute announced the creation of a new website – NGOWatch.org – to monitor the operations, funding and agendas of world society actors.[17]

The diffusion of normative agency

When Krauthammer implored the United States to embrace its power by 'unashamedly laying down the rules of world order and being prepared to enforce them',[18] he was advancing a claim about normative agency, about how the rules of international society can and should be established. This claim consists of three interlinked ideas: that the United States is, or can be, a supreme normative agent; that normative agency involves (at the hard end) issuing commands and (at the soft end) exuding cultural magnetism; and that the United States has a right, even obligation, to exercise normative agency so understood.

As noted above, the United States exercised considerable normative agency in the post-1945 period, albeit within a framework of pre-existing architectural norms. But it is interesting to note that even at this high point of American hegemony, Washington exercised a quite different form of normative agency than that advocated by neoconservatives. Within the relatively restricted confines of post-war international society, American policy-makers understood normative agency to be a form of negotiation, not command. They understood that only through dialogue could rules with social purchase ever be established. And they understood the negotiation of rules involved embedding American power, not simply wielding it. These understandings were part of America's post-war commitment to multilateralism. This commitment shaped American diplomacy in crucial areas, affecting the general structure of the United Nations, the nature of the Bretton Woods institutions and the security politics of NATO.[19] On the last of these, Steve Weber observes that 'U.S. policymakers did what they could to foster multilateralism within the alliance. Specifically, at critical points of decision, they took steps that were either most consistent with those principles or least damaging to them, given the exigencies of deterrence.'[20]

In the post-1945 period, therefore, the United States had unrivalled power resources, and was operating within a relatively confined and autonomous international society, yet it failed to embrace the neo-conservatives' Procrustean mode of normative agency. In contrast, the Bush Administration has internalized this view of normative agency, but is operating within a far more complex global social order. In the previous section, we saw how international society has become increasingly embedded in the forces and processes of world society. One aspect of this embedding is the diffusion of normative agency, that is, the increase in the range of social actors who have the capacity to shape the normative agenda, propagate new international norms and affect the interpretation of existing ones.

This increase should not be exaggerated. Sovereign states still enjoy advantageous legal prerogatives and status; some great powers retain structural advantages, such as their Security Council veto; and the United States has a broader spectrum of political resources than the current Administration appreciates. The fact is, however, that states great and small must now negotiate a world in which other actors can place issues on the international agenda, conscript international public opinion behind new normative projects, and delimit the moral terrain in which states exercise their jurisdiction domestically and pursue their interests internationally. The campaign to outlaw anti-personnel landmines, the creation of the International Criminal Court and the failure of the Multilateral Agreement on Investment are celebrated examples of such agency. Neo-conservatives often insist that American power is evident in Washington's capacity to force issues on to the international agenda, as it did in the Security Council with the issue of Iraq. But just as other states have had to respond to this initiative, so too has Washington had to engage in frenetic, yet largely unsuccessful, diplomatic activity to destroy the International Criminal Court.

Challenges of a global order

The preceding discussion suggests that the neo-conservatives' master analogy is deeply flawed. The United States certainly has a significant degree of material preponderance today, just as it did fifty years ago. But the context in which it must translate these resources into political influence is radically different. The other major powers are no longer as dependent on the United States for their existential security; they share only a thin sense of common threat; economic interdependence among major states is the order of the day, not dependence; the institutional environment is pre-structured and denser; international society is deeply penetrated by world society; and there has been a significant diffusion of normative agency. If this were not enough to complicate Washington's task, the international community now faces a number of deep systemic challenges, challenges that derive from the global consolidation of two phenomena: the system of sovereign states, and the liberal market economy. These consolidations have had a number of significant side-effects that pose profound challenges for global governance: in particular, the 'domestication' of war; the persistent maldistribution of global wealth; and the crisis in the global ecosystem. Each of these poses serious collective action problems for the community of states, as no state can escape their consequences (not even the United States), extensive cooperation is needed to address them and narrow self-interest makes such cooperation difficult to achieve.

Globalization of states and liberal economics

Commentators often counterpose globalization and the state, casting the former as a secular process antithetical to the latter. One of the most remarkable aspects of globalization, however, has been the globalization of the system of states itself, which has in turn provided a political architecture for global capitalism and communications, etc. For the first time in world history, the entire globe is divided into centralized, territorially demarcated political units, each claiming exclusive jurisdictional rights within their boundaries. The great empires of the past have disintegrated; the remaining city-states are historical anomalies. All of this has happened in the last fifty years, largely through the wholesale dissolution of the European empires. In that time we have gone from a world of around fifty states to almost 200. The global triumph of the state is thus as much a mark of globalization as that of the transnational corporation.

This triumph was the product of two forces: political and military struggle, and the politics of international law. With regard to the first of these, the early modern states of Europe emerged out of violent competition between local political elites and their internal and external rivals. War, as Charles Tilly reminds us, created states. Of course, just as this process was occurring, European sovereigns were extending global tentacles, establishing colonies first in the Americas and then in the Asia-Pacific and Africa. This too was a violent process, as Tzvetan Todorov's *The Conquest of America* reveals ever so starkly.[21] The heyday of this hybrid sovereign/imperial order was short-lived, however, spanning little more than the last decades of the nineteenth century. After that European states fell into near terminal warfare and anti-colonial nationalists fought for decolonization, sometimes embracing non-violence, sometimes not. As this history of violent state formation unfolded, international law was implicated at each stage. It was law that sanctified the principle of sovereignty at the Peace of Westphalia and that of Utrecht, and it was law that licensed European imperialism through 'the standard of civilization'.[22] It was also law, however, that ultimately delegitimated imperialism. First-wave post-colonial states used their new-found influence in the United Nations to graft the right to self-determination to emergent human rights norms, and once this graft was established the moral and legal foundations of European colonialism collapsed.[23] Since then legal principles such as sovereign equality, non-intervention and self-determination have stabilized the newly triumphant system of states, foreclosing previous options of territorial conquest and succession.

These political developments have been paralleled by the globalization of liberal market economics, a process with practical and ideational dimensions. The practical dimension is well recognized. Since the Second World War the volume of world trade has greatly increased, complemented by the transnationalization of production. This has been matched since the late 1970s by the accelerating rate of global financial flows, stimulated by the trend from fixed to floating exchange-rate regimes. It has also been matched by the dramatic increase in foreign direct investment flows. All of this has been augmented by recent revolutions in global communications and information technology. While there is some debate about whether or not current levels of economic interdependence outstrip those of the late nineteenth century, few contest the magnitude of change since the late 1940s and most acknowledge the heightened political significance of economic interdependence, given the centrality of economic management to the modern state's rationale.

The ideational dimension of liberal economic globalization is less familiar. Although economists speak of liberalization as the natural order of things, and politicians present globalization as an unstoppable force to which their societies must adapt, this merely highlights the thoroughgoing victory of liberal economic ideas. There have been three key moments in this victory. The first was after the Second World War when liberal principles informed the construction of the Bretton Woods institutions, albeit modified to accommodate European concerns to maintain full employment. The second was the 1980s victory of neoclassical economics over Keynesianism in the major industrialized states, a victory symbolized by the advent of Thatcherism in Britain. The third also occurred in the 1980s when '[v]irtually everywhere, developing countries began restructuring the nature of their intervention in the domestic economy, liberalizing their domestic trade and investment regimes, privatizing state-owned enterprises, and pursuing a variety of economic reforms more generally'.[24] By the beginning of the twenty-first century, the Third World's campaign for a New International Economic Order was dead, and liberal economics had become a global orthodoxy.

This orthodoxy, and the practices it licenses and engenders, has been consolidated by three forces. The first one concerns the structural features of economic globalization itself. The global market it has generated provides incentives and constraints for economic and political actors; networks of trade, production and financial interaction rest on routinized, normatively sanctioned practices that confront individual actors as systemic realities; and the ideology of free market capitalism has so colonized the imagination that alternatives are seldom considered. The second concerns the role of states themselves. Not only were the actions of states necessary to establish the international institutional foundations for liberal market economics after the Second World War, but continued institutional innovation has been required by states at the international level, together with energetic policies of adjustment domestically. Of course, this is a familiar story of structure and agency: structures only exist because of the routinized practices of agents, but they nevertheless confront agents as non-negotiable parameters of action. The third consolidating force has concerned international economic institutions and organizations. States create institutions to regularize international conduct, and this is precisely what institutions such as the GATT (and then the WTO) have done; they embed international economic relations in a system of socially sanctioned, increasingly enforced, rules and norms. International organizations, such as the World Bank and the International Monetary Fund, were created by states to maintain the health of the liberal market economy, and over time they have become powerful disciplinary agents, corralling state policies (particularly in the developing world) within confined neoclassical parameters.

Three side-effects

Although the state and the market have been portrayed historically as means to realize existential goals of security and prosperity, the global consolidation of the system of sovereign states and liberal market economics has had a number of central consequences that now pose profound challenges for international order and governance. The first of these is *the 'domestication' of war*, a term that captures both the taming of inter-state war and the growing relative importance of national and transnational civil violence. In the history of modern international society three forms of organized violence have predominated: the inter-state violence of territorial competition; the intra-state violence of state construction; and the revisionist violence of anti-systemic movements. The first of these has long been considered the principal threat to international order, with the devastation of the Napoleonic Wars, the First World War and the Second World War stamped on human consciousness. This inter-state violence has been paralleled, however, by a second, equally devastating form – the violence committed by political elites against their own populations as they have sought to bolster their legitimacy through the construction of ethnically homogeneous states. Here our consciousness is shaped by the Armenian genocide, the Nazi Holocaust, the Cambodian genocide, the Rwandan genocide and ethnic cleansing in the former Yugoslavia. If the horrors of these two forms of violence were not enough, the modern international system has also witnessed a third form – that employed by revisionist groups seeking to fragment existing states, challenge particular regimes and oppose structures of formal or informal imperialism. Often animated by long-standing grievances against the established domestic or international order, groups ranging from local secessionists to transnational religious fundamentalists have exercised violence to destabilize existing governments and institutions they deem illegitimate.

Over the past fifty years an important shift has occurred in the balance between these different forms of organized violence. As the global system of states has stabilized and consolidated, the incidence and scale of traditional inter-state war has declined dramatically. This is largely because of the robustness of the core norms of international society, such as non-intervention and self-determination. But it is also because of the transition of the great powers into trading states, the advent of nuclear deterrence, the codification of norms of weapons non-use and the laws of war. While the possibility of such conflict in the future remains, its probability is now considerably lower than at any other point in the history of modern international society. This has not meant, however, that organized violence has disappeared from world politics; rather, the balance has shifted towards the intra-state violence of state construction and revisionist, anti-systemic violence. There has been some progress in the codification of international norms proscribing the former, particularly when it comes to crimes against humanity and genocide, and there now exist fledgling international judicial institutions to uphold these norms, most notably the International Criminal Court. It is clear, however, that the institutional capacity to enforce norms lags well behind the development of the norms themselves, with the international community's failure to intervene in Rwanda, and its haphazard involvement in the former Yugoslavia, testimony to this lag. It is with respect to revisionist, anti-systemic violence, though, that the creation of international constraints has been most limited and least effective. There is one overriding reason for this – the political and legal framework of modern international society is designed to stabilize not just any international or world order, but a post-colonial one, in which the majority of states were built on the foundations of former colonial units. Much of the revisionist, anti-systemic violence today challenges the boundaries and political make-up of these states, and is thus directly at odds with the norms stabilizing international society.

Charles Tilly, the eminent theorist of the state, once observed that the state may be following the path of other historical institutions: just as it reaches its apogee, it begins to decline.[25] Strong versions of this proposition – that the state is dead, sovereignty is eroding, we are witnessing a new medievalism – are overdrawn. For the foreseeable future, sovereign states of various complexions are likely to remain the world's principal political institutions. There is, however, another sense in which Tilly's suggestion is illuminating. The stabilization and consolidation of the system of states has, ironically, produced the most closed political order in human history. There is now very little scope for the political revision of polities and boundaries through established legal and institutional mechanisms, which means that revisionist impulses (which are many in the post-colonial order) seek illegitimate means, often violent ones.

The second side-effect is *the persistent maldistribution of global wealth.* When Francis Fukuyama proclaimed the end of history over a decade ago, criticisms were legion. But while serious philosophical and empirical inquiry found his ideas wanting, many in the West deeply internalized them ideologically. The collapse of the Soviet Union and the liberation of its Eastern European clients was seen as a victory for liberalism and capitalism, and the remarkable period of economic growth experienced by the United States during the 1990s encouraged a sense, at the core of the international system, that the key to managing global capitalism had been found. As people in the West grew confident in their ever more affluent lifestyles, it was quietly assumed that this was a global trend that could be further accelerated simply by the opening up of global markets and the deregulation of national economies. As the Bush Administration repeatedly insists, one 'single sustainable model of national success' prevails.

The political problem for the international community is that there is a profound gap between the belief, well-founded or otherwise, that liberal market economics can eventually deliver global economic well-being and the lived experience of many of the world's peoples, an experience that is unlikely to shift substantially in any politically relevant time span. Let us consider the following. In 1998 the World Bank estimated that 1,214 million people (out of the global population of 5,820 million) were living below the international poverty line.[26] At the beginning of the new millennium, the United Nations Development Program calculated that 14 per cent of the world's people were undernourished, 16 per cent lacked access to safe drinking water and 40 per cent lacked basic sanitation.[27] In 2001 the *World Heath Report* concluded that one-third of all human deaths were due to poverty-related causes. Thomas Pogge writes that if 'the developed Western countries had their proportional shares of these deaths, severe poverty would kill some 3,500 Britons and 16,500 Americans per week'.[28] Global trends are at best mixed. The most recent *Human Development Report* notes that people living in extreme poverty fell from 29 per cent in 1990 to 23 per cent in 1999, but in sub-Saharan Africa the number rose from 242 million to 300 million.[29] At the same time, the gap between the world's richest citizens and the poorest further widened. In 1990 the gap between the fifth living in the richest countries and the fifth living in the poorest was 60 to 1 – by 1997 it had grown to 74 to 1.[30]

The potential for this gap between the promise of economic globalization and the lived experience of such a large sector of the world's population to generate disorder and violence should not be underestimated. Furthermore, this potential is exacerbated by the closed political structures encountered by many of the world's poor. This has two dimensions. First, as the World Bank and the United Nations Development Program now emphasize, economic collapse and failed political institutions often go hand in hand, which means that in many states there are no effective institutional mechanisms for the expression, let alone satisfaction, of economic grievances. Second, even where trademark democratic institutions exist, the scope for democratic oversight of national economic policy is often severely limited. In fact, the coercive apparatus of developing states is frequently deployed to enforce the economic adjustment strategies prescribed by international financial institutions.

The third effect is *the crisis in the global ecosystem*. The symptoms of this crisis are familiar. The United Nations Environment Program's report, *Global Environment Outlook: 2000*, paints a grim picture of widespread environmental degradation and pervasive political inaction. 'Full-scale emergencies' now exist in the following areas, to name but a few: the world's water cycle is now in such a condition that it will soon be unable to cope with human needs; land degradation and desertification are outpacing advances in agricultural technologies and techniques; the destruction of tropical forests 'has gone too far to prevent irreversible damage'; a quarter of all mammalian species and over 10 per cent of bird species are at serious risk of extinction; air pollution has reached 'crisis dimensions' in many urban areas, with major public health implications; and it 'is probably too late to prevent global warming as a result of increased greenhouse gas emissions'.[31] Despite the fact that it is now almost thirty years since the agenda-setting 1972 Stockholm Conference and nearly ten years since the Rio Summit, the report concludes that 'the global system of environmental management is moving in the right direction but much too slowly.... If the new millennium is not to be marred by major environmental disasters, alternative policies will have to be swiftly implemented.'[32]

Localized human-induced environmental devastation pre-dates the globalization of the system of states and liberal market economics, but the current global environmental crisis is intimately connected with these processes. First, the global consolidation of the system of sovereign states laid the foundations for an almost intractable collective action problem. No state is immune from the effects of the crisis (though some are better positioned than others); it can only be addressed effectively through collective action, and yet the narcissistic sovereignty of most states makes such cooperation profoundly difficult. Second, while market mechanisms can usefully contribute to environmental protection, the globalization of liberal market economics has simultaneously encouraged environmentally damaging modes of economic development and privileged small government paths to growth, paths that are antithetical to the proactive strategies that researchers now believe might enable sustainable growth.[33] Third, the parallel globalization of the state system and liberal market economics has produced the economic-managerial state, a state whose rationale is the maintenance of perpetual growth. In a world of such states, the collective action problem of environmental protection is profound indeed.

Together, the above side-effects constitute a triad of disorder. The domestication of war contributes to global poverty and ecological devastation; economic deprivation is fertile soil for violent politics and unconducive to environmentally sustainable practices; and a growing body of research demonstrates the dangerous connection between ecological collapse, acute conflict and impoverishment.[34] Furthermore, this triad is a source of other contemporary transnational problems, such as refugees and unauthorized people movements, ethnic conflict and terrorism. They thus constitute fundamental and unavoidable challenges for global governance.

Conclusion

Scholars have long argued about whether Washington sought global hegemony after the Second World War, or merely leadership within the Western sphere of an emerging bipolar order. Interesting as this debate is, one thing is certain: American ambitions were severely circumscribed by two structural features of the post-war international system. The first was bipolarity. By 1948 at the latest, it was clear that the new world order would be a divided one – ideologically, politically, economically and geographically. This order both empowered the United States and Soviet Union, providing a rationale for their respective spheres of influence, and constrained them, delimiting each of their global ambitions. Over time, this bifurcation of world politics came to rest not only on mutual threats and proxy wars, but also on mutually accepted rules of the game, with the Helsinki accords that recognized Europe's post-war borders being perhaps the most noteworthy. The second constraining feature was the post-war decolonization. When the United States first emerged as pre-eminent, the society of sovereign states was small indeed, with little more than fifty recognized members, the majority of whom were European by origin. In the next three decades, international society expanded dramatically, but the scope of superpower influence was frustrated by the emerging politics of non-alignment, the campaign for the new international economic order and the expression of both of these within core international institutions, such as the United Nations. These two structural features of the post-1945 international system conspired against truly global American hegemony, despite the fact that hegemonic stability theorists wrote as though other spheres never existed.

By the beginning of the 1990s, bipolarity had gone and post-colonial self-assertiveness had faded, removing these constraints on American globalists. For the first time in history an American Administration is seeking hegemony on a global scale, a project unmatched by any other great power in history, even Rome. More importantly for our purposes, it is an order of magnitude more ambitious than the neo-conservatives' analogy with American hegemony after the Second World War would suggest. The constraints of bipolarity and post-colonial collective action may have gone, but, as we have seen on page 76, world politics is now infinitely more complex. The other great powers are no longer as dependent on the United States for their survival; their sense of a common threat is thin at best; economic interdependence is the prevailing mode of association, not dependence; the institutional order is denser and pre-structured; international society is enveloped by world society; and normative agency has diffused significantly. Added to this, we have seen that the globalization of the system of states and the liberal market economy has contributed to the domestication of war, the persistent maldistribution of global wealth and the current ecological crisis, all of which pose profound challenges to global governance. Even for a state with the material resources of the United States, one would have to conclude that seeking hegemony in such a world is a far greater challenge than when established in the more circumscribed hegemony of the immediate post-1945 order.

Unfortunately, the Bush Administration seems unaware of the magnitude of this challenge. On the geo-political front, it asserts either that 'the great powers are ... increasingly united by common values', or that the United States has the capacity to combat the rise of any challengers.[35] On the normative and institutional fronts, it imagines a world embracing America's universal values and the 'single sustainable model of national success'. As we saw in chapter 2, the Administration's view of hegemony has two dimensions: a core realist dimension in which hegemony is seen as the material capacity to 'lay down the rules', and a peripheral, yet important, 'Gramscian' dimension that stresses the role of cultural magnetism in cultivating consent. Even in the less complex international environment of the post-war world, Washington exhibited and enacted a more nuanced, less heavy-handed view of American power and influence. In today's more complex environment, a more sophisticated understanding is required, one akin to that advanced in the previous chapter. Hegemony must be seen as a form of social hierarchy, based on status and recognition. It must be cemented by generally recognized procedural and substantive norms, and these norms must reflect the negotiation of the hegemon's and other states' identities and interests. Furthermore, the hegemon must pursue its interests in a manner consistent with these norms, or the legitimacy of its leadership will fast erode. To construct such hegemony in a world as complex as today's demands a quality of statesmanship as yet unapparent in the 'gunboat' diplomacy of the Bush Administration.

4

The Ethics of Moralists

In the movie *Monty Python's Life of Brian* there is a scene in which the People's Front of Judea meet to plot the downfall of the Roman Empire. The Romans have 'bled us white', inveighs Reg, their hapless leader: 'What have they ever given us in return?' In their less than helpful way, his fellow revolutionaries go on to list a whole series of goods provided by their Roman conquerors. In the end, an increasingly frustrated Reg rephrases his condemnation: 'Alright, but apart from the sanitation, medicine, education, wine, public order, irrigation, roads, the fresh water system, and public health, what have the Romans ever done for us?'[1]

Satirical as this is, it reveals the ethical ambivalence we often feel towards the existence and exercise of dominance or hegemony in international relations. Such power can be overweening and exploitative, but it can also be essential to the realization of public goods and humanitarian goals. America's war against Iraq was condemned for being 'illegal, immoral, and illogical',[2] but Washington is criticized for not intervening in Rwanda. America's mission to spread democracy often appears imperialistic, but resonates at some level with values many endorse. America's global economic policies are blamed for the widening gulf between the rich and poor, but its role in stabilizing the world economy is acknowledged and its foreign aid desired.

How should we think about the ethics of American hegemony? Developing a comprehensive ethical theory on the topic is beyond the scope of this book, although one is sorely needed. My purpose here is to answer three more circumscribed, yet clearly related, questions: what type of hegemonic project are we seeking to evaluate, and what is the nature of the international environment in which this policy is being prosecuted? What ethical principles would be appropriate for assessing this project? And how does the Bush Doctrine rate against these principles? Addressing these questions is warranted for two reasons. To begin with, moralists invite moral scrutiny. The Bush Administration has not shied away from making moral justifications for its international posture, and it seems only reasonable to reflect on the merits of these justifications. Second, all policies that prescribe actions are informed by ethics that give these policies purpose. These might be ethics of self-interest, political order, social justice or some other values, but they are ethics nonetheless. A rounded analysis of the Bush Doctrine should thus include some consideration of this purposive dimension.

The following discussion is divided into three parts. In the first I pick up threads from previous chapters to argue that our task is to evaluate a revisionist hegemonic project being prosecuted within a highly complex global order, with distinctive structural features and challenges. I then assess existing arguments about the moral basis of hegemony, focusing primarily on the contending propositions that: might is right; might is right if it preserves international order; might is right if it serves cosmopolitan values; might is right if it is liberal; and might is never right. The first and last of these are dismissed as counterintuitive: few would argue that the exercise of power is subject to no ethical constraints, and the idea that might can never be right conflicts with the widespread belief that a hegemon intervening to prevent genocide would be ethically justified. From the remaining arguments I distil four ethical principles for evaluating the Bush Administration's revisionist project. The final part of the chapter employs these principles to critique the Administration's moral justifications and grand strategy.

Revisionist politics in a complex global order

In seeking to assess the ethics of the Bush Administration's grand strategy, I am not seeking to evaluate the ethics of dominance or hegemony in general, although this clearly has a bearing on what I have to say. My task is the more specific one of assessing a radical project of hegemonic renewal, a project that seeks to reassert American dominance and to transform world order in the process. As we have seen, this is a project being pursued within an increasingly complex global order. Before proceeding, it is worth briefly reviewing the nature of the Administration's grand strategy, as well as the complexities of the present order.

Neo-conservatives within and outside the Bush Administration cast the United States in the role of Machiavelli's new prince, the autocratic founder who uses his power to establish the foundations of a successful state. Machiavelli writes that it 'rarely or never happens that a republic or kingdom is well organized from the beginning, or completely reformed...unless it is done by one man alone; moreover, it is necessary that one man provide the means and be the only one from whose mind any such organization originates.'[3] For neo-conservatives, the international system is once again on the brink of disorder, and the United States is the only viable force against entropy. As we saw in the previous chapter, Bush declared that 'this nation and our friends are all that stand between a world at peace, and a world of chaos and alarm'.[4] The Administration's vision, however, is more than simply shoring up the status quo; it is a creative project of unilateral reformation. Its purported goals are the spread of freedom, democracy and free enterprise, and, while these received a substantial boost with the end of the Cold War, they are now challenged by the alliance of global terrorism and rogue states supposedly armed with weapons of mass destruction. Realizing its vision while combating these challenges is said to demand fundamental revisions to the way in which the United States conducts its international relations, from the nature of its military-strategic posture and the rules governing covert operations to the laws of war and its relationship to international institutions. All must adapt to allow the successful prosecution of the Administration's grand strategy. Not only does this project pose a fundamental challenge to the established framework of global governance, it involves 'in detail and in gross, a rejection of previous standards and doctrines that have long defined American statecraft and diplomacy'.[5] That Washington's goals appear liberal, but its means illiberal, fits well with the mould of Machiavelli's new prince: bold autocratic actions were necessary to found a viable state, even a republic of free citizens.

This project of hegemonic renewal is being pursued in an international environment more complex and challenging than at any other point in international history. After the Second World War Washington pursued an ambitious project of hegemonic construction, but it did so within an international environment in which the non-communist great powers were critically dependent on it for their security and economic reconstruction, in which the institutional architecture of international society was weak and other states were open to its redevelopment, in which international society remained relatively autonomous from world society, and in which normative agency was largely, though not exclusively, a state preserve. This world was not only more amenable to hegemonic construction than today's, but was also more amenable to certain ethical defences of hegemony. For instance, arguments about rights of self-defence could easily be collectivized, as the non-communist powers had similar threat perceptions. Likewise, arguments that stressed America's role in the provision of international public goods were easier to sustain, as the requisite goods revolved around the maintenance of order within what remained a relatively conventional society of sovereign states, wracked though it was by the Cold War. As the previous chapter demonstrates, the environment in which the Bush Administration is prosecuting its hegemonic project is radically different from this mid-twentieth century context. Everything, from the structure of security dependence to the distribution of normative agency, has altered in significant ways. Beyond this, though, the globalization of the system of states and the liberal market economy has produced a triad of profound collective action problems; namely, the domestication of war, the persistent maldistribution of global wealth and the crisis in the global ecosystem. This world places multiple obstacles before a revisionist project of hegemonic renewal, not the least being the problem of justification. Claims of self-defence may well justify sporadic military campaigns, but not wholesale tutelage; and claims about the provision of public goods will have to meet collective, not unilateral, understandings of what those goods might be in a world such as this.

Existing arguments

What are the ethical arguments currently available to assess the Bush Administration's revisionist grand strategy? For many, the only ethical position possible in international relations is the principle that might equals right. This principle was articulated by the Athenian generals in the Melian Dialogue of Thucydides' *History of the Peloponnesian War*. Athens sent a force to invade the island of Melos, which had refused to join the empire and tried to remain neutral, despite the fact that it was a Spartan colony. Athens dispatched its generals to negotiate with the Melians before invading, and their speech has become one of the most infamous expressions of the principle that might equals right:

> [W]e on our side will use no fine phrases saying, for example, that we have a right to our empire because we defeated the Persians, or that we come against you now because of the injuries you have done us – a great mass of words nobody would believe.... [T]he standard of justice depends on the equality of power to compel and that in fact the strong do what they have the power to do and the weak accept what they have to accept.[6]

This ethical position consists of four interrelated ideas: that ethical principles can only exist, or have any relevance, if there is power to enforce them; that in relations between states there is no central power to enforce universal ethical principles; that in such a world, the power of particular states upholds their particular values; and that, as a consequence, there can be no ethical standpoint from which to critique the ethical claims of the powerful. From this perspective, the Bush Administration's grand strategy can only ever be just, as there is no more overarching site of power in contemporary international relations from which enforceable principles might emanate.

The second, frequently invoked, ethical position is that hegemony is justified if the dominant state provides international public goods. These are goods that all members of international society can 'consume' or benefit from, irrespective of whether they, as individual states, have helped bear the costs of their provision.[7] Commonly cited examples are a stable balance of power, freedom of the high seas and open international markets. One version of this position is articulated by pluralist international society theorists. Hedley Bull argued that states share three elementary goals of social life: that they will be secure against violence, that promises will be kept and that their territorial property rights will be respected. Only when these elementary goals are sustained can we say that international order exists. But how can these be sustained in a world without central authority? Bull identifies several sources of international order – including international law, diplomacy and even war – but he also stresses the special role of great powers. If states were all equal in power, Bull wondered how 'international conflicts could ever be settled and laid to rest, or the claims of any one state definitely granted or denied'.[8] The existence of great powers, however, allows the establishment of a modicum of order. 'Great powers contribute to international order in two main ways: by managing their relations with one another; and by exploiting their preponderance in such a way as to impart a degree of central direction to the affairs of international society as a whole.'[9] Bull denied that a great power-sponsored order could ever be perfectly just, but he clearly saw this order, and the role of great powers in sustaining it, as ethically justifiable. Order was, in Bull's mind, a prerequisite for justice, and he thus held that 'order is desirable, or valuable in human affairs, and *a fortiori* in world politics'.[10]

Another version of the public goods argument is articulated by hegemonic stability theorists. Behind this version lies a simple proposition drawn from economic theory: 'even if all of the individuals in a large group are rational and self-interested, and would gain if, as a group, they acted to achieve their common interest or objective, they will still not voluntarily act to achieve that common or group interest'.[11] In the context of international relations, this means that even if states would all benefit from the provision of certain public goods, they may not voluntarily act to realize those goods. The reason for this is that 'individuals are likely to calculate that they are better off by not contributing, since their contribution is costly to them but has an imperceptible effect on whether the good is produced'.[12] If all states think like this, then the public goods in question will never be provided. That is, unless a hegemonic state is prepared to bear the costs of providing such goods. Hegemonic stability theorists claim that hegemons have strong incentives to do this, as they stand to gain most from geo-political stability, open markets, etc. Certainly the actions of Britain in the nineteenth century and the United States after the Second World War bear this out, as both helped provide significant public goods for international society. The inter-war period, in contrast, is often cited as evidence of the disorder that can result when there is no hegemonic power to sustain international order; the lack of a leading state to manage the world economy, for example, is seen as a principal cause of the Great Depression.[13] From this perspective, therefore, the exercise of hegemonic power can be justified if it delivers international public goods. Nye argues that American foreign policy should be redirected to the provision of such goods, partly because it would serve America's national interests, and partly because it would bolster its international legitimacy.[14] Advocates of this position rarely use explicit ethical language, but any justification that ties the provision of social goods to legitimacy is inescapably normative in nature and intent.

The third possible ethical position holds that might is right if it furthers cosmopolitan ends, such as promoting international human rights or facilitating global distributive justice. A hegemon is to be judged not on the basis of whether it provides order among sovereign states – or at least not primarily – but with regard to its success or failure in protecting the rights and satisfying the needs of individual human beings. Surprisingly, there are few well-elaborated statements of this position, despite the fact that it is implied in many critiques of American foreign policy, today and in the past. Henry Shue's classic work *Basic Rights* comes close to such a statement, making the case as it does that American foreign policy ought to prioritize the promotion of certain 'subsistence rights'. But Shue stops short of arguing that American hegemony would be justified by the provision of such rights, even if he might believe this.[15] We are left, therefore, to anticipate the main contours of such an argument. Given the general principles of cosmopolitan thought, four interrelated ideas seem relevant. First, individuals not states are the proper *locus* of ethical concern. Second, institutions of power are only justified if they uphold the rights and fulfil the needs of said individuals. Third, because the world is practically interdependent, it is morally interdependent as well. And finally, hegemony, as an institution of power, is justified only if it helps to defend the rights and satisfy the needs of individuals living in this morally interdependent world. This final idea might have negative and positive dimensions. An ethically defensible hegemon would have to refrain from violating individuals' rights or compromising their needs, but it would also be obliged, given the reach of its power and the benefits it gains from such reach, to be proactive when states or markets fail.

The fourth ethical defence of hegemony draws on traditional liberal political values. Both the second and third of our justifications invoked liberal themes, such as the ideas that political institutions are legitimate if they provide public goods or uphold the rights of individuals. A number of authors have gone further, though, in articulating an explicit liberal justification for the exercise of dominant state power. A case in point is Lea Brilmayer's *American Hegemony: Political Morality in a One-Superpower World*. Brilmayer argues that hegemony must be seen as a form of governance, a political institution that ought to be judged on the same basis as domestic political institutions. This is not only because a hegemon sits at the apex of a hierarchy of power, just as the state does, but because like the state a hegemon provides public goods. It follows, therefore, that 'it should be evaluated *as though* the hegemon were a world government of comparable capacities and engaged in comparable activities'.[16] As a liberal, Brilmayer believes that such an evaluation should be based on two principles common to all liberal theories. 'The first is the emphasis on democratic participation, with governance resting on some form of popular consent. The second is the protection of a particular set of substantive human rights from oppression even by majorities.'[17] Most of Brilmayer's book is devoted to addressing the myriad of problems raised by trying to apply the first of these standards to power in international relations. The concept of consent has always been a bugbear for liberal political theorists, and its problems are only amplified in international relations. Is it states or individuals that need to consent to hegemony? Is consent needed for all hegemonic acts, or only for hegemonic rule in general? Under what conditions should consent be seen as freely given? Is bribery-induced consent genuine? Does tacit consent count, and if so, how does one know when it has been given? Brilmayer's answers to these questions are more statist than cosmopolitan. The exercise of hegemonic power is ethically justifiable if it rests on the consent of weaker states, but to ensure that these states truly represent the interests of their peoples, the hegemon itself must assess those interests. 'This means, in practice, that the interests of people in other states (as best we guess them) must be a check on our agreements with their governments.'[18]

The final ethical position – the polar opposite of the first – holds that the exercise of hegemonic power is never ethically justifiable. One source of such a position might be pacifist thought, which abhors the use of violence even in unambiguous cases of self-defence. This would not, however, provide a comprehensive critique of the exercise of hegemonic power, which takes forms other than overt violence, such as economic diplomacy or the manipulation of international institutions. A more likely source of such critique would be the multifarious literature that equates all power with domination. Postmodernists (and anarchists, for that matter) might argue that behind all power lies self-interest and a will to control, both of which are antithetical to genuine human freedom and diversity. Radical liberals might contend that the exercise of power by one human over another transforms the latter from a moral agent into a moral subject, thus violating their integrity as self-governing individuals. Whatever the source, these ideas lead to radical scepticism about all institutions of power, of which hegemony is one form. The idea that the state is a source of individual security is replaced here with the idea of the state as a tyranny; the idea of hegemony as essential to the provision of global public goods is replaced with the idea of dominant power as inimical to the human good.

A framework for judgement

Which of the above ideas help us to evaluate the ethics of the Bush Administration's revisionist hegemonic project? There is a strong temptation in international relations scholarship to mount trenchant defences of favoured paradigms, to show that the core assumptions of one's preferred theory can be adapted to answer an ever widening set of big and important questions. There is a certain discipline of mind that this cultivates, and it certainly brings some order to theoretical debates, but it can lead to the 'Cinderella syndrome', the squeezing of an ungainly, over-complicated world into an undersized theoretical glass slipper. The study of international ethics is not immune this syndrome, with a long line of scholars seeking master normative principles of universal applicability. My approach here is a less ambitious, more pragmatic one. With the exceptions of the first and last positions, each of the above ethical perspectives contains kernels of wisdom. The challenge is to identify those of value for evaluating the ethics of Bush's revisionist grand strategy, and to consider how they might stand in order of priority. The following discussion takes up this challenge and arrives at a position that I tentatively term 'procedural solidarism'.

The first and last of our five ethical positions can be dismissed as unhelpful to our task. The idea that might is right resonates with the cynical attitude we often feel towards the darker aspects of international relations, but it does not constitute an ethical standpoint from which to judge the exercise of hegemonic power. First of all, it places the right of moral judgement in the hands of the hegemon, and leaves all of those subject to its actions with no grounds for ethical critique. What the hegemon dictates as ethical is ethical. More than this, though, the principle that might is right is undiscriminating. It gives us no resources to determine ethical from unethical hegemonic conduct. The idea that might is never right is equally unsatisfying. It is a principle implied in many critiques of imperial power, including of American power. But like its polar opposite, it is utterly undiscriminating. No matter what the hegemon does we are left with one blanket assessment. No procedure, no selfless goal is worthy of ethical endorsement. This is a deeply impoverished ethical posture, as it raises the critique of power above all other human values. It is also completely counter-intuitive. Had the United States intervened militarily to prevent the Rwandan genocide, would this not have been ethically justifiable? If one answers no, then one faces the difficult task of explaining why the exercise of hegemonic power would have been a greater evil than allowing almost a million people to be massacred. If one answers yes, then one is admitting that a more discriminating set of ethical principles is needed than the simple yet enticing proposition that might is never right.

Three kernels of wisdom

The second, third and fourth of our ethical positions each contain compelling propositions. The idea that the exercise of hegemonic power is justified if the state in question provides international public goods is difficult to deny. At all points in international history it has been possible to identify public goods that need to be provided if a modicum of order is to be realized and sustained. In the nineteenth century, ensuring a stable balance of power between the great powers was recognized as essential to reducing inter-state violence, and in the same period states regarded the eradication of piracy as necessary for the development of imperial and international trade. In the twentieth century, a stable balance of power between the superpowers, an effective network of international institutions and open international markets have all been valued as desirable public goods. If it is indeed true that the leadership of a dominant state, or the collaboration of a number of great powers, is necessary to realize these goods, then one could presumably marshal a compelling ethical defence of a state that used its power in such a way. To counter such a defence, it would be necessary to show that the goods in question were not actually goods, that the costs of their provision outweighed the benefits, or that there were other more desirable ways of achieving them than through the actions of a dominant state.

The idea that hegemonic power is ethically justifiable if it is used in the service of cosmopolitan ends is also compelling. It is not necessary to argue here that ends such as the protection and promotion of international human rights or the fostering of global distributive justice are universal values, only that in one form or another they have been enshrined as international norms. The issue of human rights is the least problematic. It is now generally accepted that state sovereignty is not an unequivocal right, and that states have obligations to protect the basic human rights of their peoples. It is also accepted that the international community has a role to play in promoting such rights and in combating the most egregious violations. To argue against these propositions would be to swim against the tide of international opinion. The case of global distributive justice is slightly more difficult. Strong norms exist in the international system that rich industrialized countries have obligations to provide foreign aid to poorer countries, although state performance in this area varies enormously.[19] There is also a complex of international institutions devoted to poverty alleviation and economic development, the most notable being the United Nations Development Program and the World Bank. At best, these developments point to a thin norm of distributive justice, but it is nonetheless a rather robust and historically unique norm. At no other point in international history has such a norm existed – let alone a framework of associated institutions – and few would accept the contrary proposition that the global rich have no obligations to the global poor, although some indeed make this argument. It seems reasonable, therefore, to argue that a dominant state that used its capacities to further these cosmopolitan goals would be ethically defensible.

Finally, the idea that the exercise of a dominant state's power is justifiable if it is based on the consent of those affected has clear merit. Jean-Jacques Rousseau famously wrote that free, equal and reciprocal 'agreements remain the basis of all legitimate authority among men',[20] but until the middle of the nineteenth century this was a revolutionary idea. Since then, however, the proposition that the exercise of political power must be based on consent has become the touchstone of political legitimacy. The limits of representative democracy are frequently enumerated, but governments in modern democracies claim legitimacy on the grounds that their rule is based on the consent of the people. Conversely, autocracy is condemned for lacking such consent. In the international arena, a cardinal principle of international law is that states are bound only by rules to which they have consented, although the binding nature of customary law greatly complicates this. The notion that consent is a prerequisite for the legitimate exercise of political power has thus been thoroughly naturalized. We are left, however, with a difficult set of questions about whose consent is required to authorize particular forms of power, and about what constitutes genuine consent. But these questions aside, the idea advanced by Brilmayer that hegemonic power might be justified if it is based on the consent of those subject to it is both intuitively plausible and resonates with prevailing norms of political rule.

A pragmatic synthesis

Endorsing the above ideas is relatively easy. Determining which should have priority and how they should relate to one another is far more difficult. The problem stems from the fact that the provision of international public goods, the pursuit of cosmopolitan ends and the requirement of consent are not necessarily compatible. It may be that the pursuit of one demands the deferment or sacrifice of another. This is the issue that animates the persistent debate about the relationship between order and justice in international relations. Bull's original position was that order must take priority, that it is 'only if there is a pattern of social activity in which elementary or primary goals of social life are in some degree provided for, that advanced or secondary goals can be secured'.[21] More than this, however, he believed that the mechanisms used to preserve international order were inimical to the pursuit of justice. The balancing of power, war, international law and management by the great powers all 'systematically affront the most basic and widely agreed principles of international justice'.[22] This view is countered by those who believe that justice is in fact a prerequisite for order, and that political systems marred by deep injustices are prone to conflict and instability. Bull himself came close to this view later in life. As the European empires decolonized and a 'Third World coalition' emerged with demands for equity and distributive justice, Bull feared that failure to address these demands might erode the foundations of international order.[23] My own resolution of this dilemma – pragmatic and partial though it is – is to suggest: (1) the normative priority of cosmopolitan ends; (2) the practical inseparability of order and justice; and (3) the prudential priority of institutionally governed change.

There is an essential truth, I believe, in John Rawls' claim that '[e]ach person possesses an inviolability founded on justice that even the welfare of society cannot override'.[24] For the past two or three centuries we have used the language of human rights to speak of this inviolability. All individuals, regardless of nationality, race, colour, sex or religion, possess certain basic rights, particularly to subsistence, security and liberty. These rights, Shue contends, 'are the rational basis for justified demands the denial of which no self-respecting person can reasonably be expected to accept'.[25] As noted earlier (page 116), human rights have moved beyond the confines of philosophical treatises to become litmus tests of political legitimacy. Human rights are violated every day on every continent, but offending states must hide and deny these violations. Governments still invoke the principle of sovereignty to shield themselves from outside scrutiny, but this is no longer a persuasive rhetorical shield. The International Bill of Rights – which encompasses the Universal Declaration and the Covenants on Civil and Political Rights and Social and Economic Rights – sets out core and ancillary international human rights, as well as the legal obligations incumbent on states. These instruments also impose obligations on the international community – obligations that are presently expanding, from the promotion of international human rights and the enhancement of state capacities, to intervention in cases of gross state abuse and international prosecution for crimes against humanity and genocide.

Cosmopolitan values, such as international human rights, may well have normative priority, but in practice they are entwined with traditional values of order in international society. The provision of order in international relations is an abiding common interest of states, and they have gone to considerable lengths to enshrine ordering principles, such as sovereignty, non-intervention and self-determination, and rules governing the use of force. They have also put considerable energy into the construction and maintenance of institutions to uphold these principles: institutions such as international law, multilateralism and universal conferences of states. Pluralist scholars of international society frequently present these developments as though they have been cognitively, discursively and practically quarantined from wider ethical discourses. Nothing could be further from the truth, however. The meaning and implications of the principle of sovereignty have always been informed by ideas of legitimate statehood, which in the modern era have been increasingly tied to cosmopolitan values such as individual rights. Similarly, the international institutions that states have created over the past two centuries are not merely functional constructions, but are (albeit imperfect) embodiments of liberal governance values, such as the principles that consent is the only legitimate basis of law and that rules must apply equally to all. Over time these institutions have also become vehicles for the promotion of such values domestically. An interesting example of this is the clear, if controversial, broadening of the meaning of 'threats to international peace and security' under the United Nations' Charter to encompass humanitarian crises. At each of these levels, the politics of order has been entwined with that of justice, the provision of traditional public goods with that of cosmopolitan ends.

Saying that order and justice are practically entwined is not the same as saying that their interrelationship is unproblematic. Elsewhere, I have referred to the 'anxiety of international politics', and one of the principal sources of that anxiety is the perpetual difficulty of reconciling these two goods.[26] While cosmopolitan values have gained unprecedented normative standing in contemporary international society, they are realized only partially, with egregious violations of basic rights blotting the copybooks of many states. Are there limits to the actions states should take to stamp out these violations, individually or collectively? Is military intervention justified to overthrow tyranny or to alleviate famine if it risks an escalation of local and international violence, or if it violates the established ordering principles and institutional practices of international society? Questions such as these led Bull to conclude that 'terrible choices have sometimes to be made'.[27]

My preference here is to advocate a forward-leaning, prudential strategy of institutionally governed change. By 'forward-leaning', I mean that the progressive realization of cosmopolitan values should be the measure of successful politics in international society. As long as gross violations of basic human rights mar global social life, we, as individuals, and the states that purport to represent us, have obligations to direct what political influence we have to the improvement of the human condition, both at home and abroad. I recommend, however, that our approach be prudent rather than imprudent. Historically, the violence of inter-state warfare and the oppression of imperial rule have been deeply corrosive of basic human rights across the globe. The institutions of international society, along with their constitutive norms, such as sovereignty, non-intervention, self-determination and limits on the use of force, have helped to reduce these corrosive forces dramatically. The incidence of inter-state wars has declined markedly, even though the number of states has multiplied, and imperialism and colonialism have moved from being core institutions of international society to practices beyond the pale. Prudence dictates, therefore, that we lean forward without losing our footing on valuable institutions and norms. This means, in effect, giving priority to institutionally governed change, working with the rules and procedures of international society rather than against them.

What does this mean in practice? In general, I take it to mean two things. First, it means recognizing the principal rules of international society, and accepting the obligations they impose on actors, including oneself. These rules fall into two broad categories: procedural and substantive. The most specific procedural rules are embodied in institutions such as the United Nations Security Council, which is empowered to 'determine the existence of any threat to peace, breach of the peace or act of aggression' and the measures that will be taken 'to maintain or restore international peace and security'.[28] More general, yet equally crucial, procedural rules include the cardinal principle that states are only bound by rules to which they have consented. Even customary international law, which binds states without their express consent, is based in part on the assumption of their tacit consent. The substantive rules of international society are legion, but perhaps the most important are the rules governing the use of force, both when force is permitted (*jus ad bellum*) and how it may be used (*jus in bello*). Second, working with the rules and procedures of international society also means recognizing that the principal modality of innovation and change must be communicative. That is, establishing new rules and mechanisms for achieving cosmopolitan ends and international public goods, or modifying existing ones, should be done through persuasion and negotiation, not ultimatum and coercion. A premium must be placed, therefore, on articulating the case for change, on recognizing the concerns and interests of others as legitimate, on building upon existing rules, and on seeing genuine communication as a process of give and take, not demand and take.

Giving priority to institutionally governed change may seem an overly conservative strategy, but it need not be. As explained above, the established procedural and substantive rules of international society have delivered international public goods that actually further cosmopolitan ends, albeit in a partial and inadequate fashion. Eroding these rules would only lead to increases in inter-state violence and imperialism, and this would almost certainly produce a radical deterioration in the protection of basic human rights across the globe. Saying that we ought to preserve these rules is prudent, not conservative. More than this, though, we have learnt that the institutions of international society have transformative potential, even if this is only now being creatively exploited.

In recent years, scholars have demonstrated two aspects of this potential. First, they have shown that state and non-state actors can establish new rules of international society by taking established principles and 'grafting' new norms on to them. For instance, anti-landmine campaigners took ideas of 'civilized' warfare that were enshrined in the Hague and Geneva Conventions and successfully argued that the manufacture and use of anti-personnel landmines contravened these ideas, thus helping to establish a new norm of non-use.[29] Second, scholars have shown that states often sign up to international human rights treaties with little commitment to seeing their norms enforced.

However, across a wide range of cases, informal networks have emerged between international organizations and human rights non-governmental organizations, working locally and transnationally. These networks generally lack material power, but they have brought about genuine change in state practices through strategies of persuasion and socialization, employing 'information politics', 'symbolic politics', 'leverage politics' and 'accountability politics'. 'No mere "enactors," these are people who seek to amplify the generative power of norms, broaden the scope of practices those norms engender, and sometimes even renegotiate or transform the norms themselves.'[30] In the hands of creative political agents, the rules of international society can thus become normative assets in a transformative politics that blurs the boundaries between international and world society.

There is, I believe, only one compelling reason for dropping the reins of prudence and pursuing cosmopolitan values outside the established institutional processes of international society – that doing so is the only way to prevent or arrest a supreme humanitarian emergency. Just as most of us would break the law to save the life of a child, so too should we be prepared to skirt international rules to prevent crimes that 'shock the moral conscience of humankind'. Over the past fifty years, scholars have swung between upholding the sanctity of the principle of non-intervention and calling for the establishment of a right to humanitarian military intervention. The former was prominent during the Vietnam War, when the dangers of superpower adventurism were plain to see; the latter rose to prominence after the end of the Cold War, when the dangers of geo-politics were momentarily eclipsed by an apparent rise in communal violence.[31] The tide now seems to be drifting back the other way, as the hubris of the strong is once again in need of constraint. The challenge is not, however, to foreclose the possibility of humanitarian military intervention, for to do so would be to abrogate our most basic duties of care. Rather, it is to reserve such interventions for situations of supreme humanitarian emergency. The threshold here must be high, otherwise the language of humanitarianism will be conscripted to serve the most self-interested of ends. I define a 'supreme humanitarian emergency' in a similar way to Michael Walzer. That is, as a situation in which a substantial number of a community's members face enslavement, massacre or starvation.[32] Intervention by this standard was justified in Somalia and Kosovo, and would certainly have been in Rwanda, although questions of implementation and effectiveness plague the first two cases.

This begs the question, though, of how we should decide that a supreme humanitarian emergency is under way. How can we be sure that the threshold has been reached, and that great powers are not simply hiding their self-interested behaviour behind the veil of humanitarianism? This seems to me to be an issue of institutional design, of establishing procedures that permit rapid action but impartial decision-making. Henry Shue's proposal for *post facto* independent review of interventions is one possible solution. It 'would take one small step to regularize unavoidable intervention, to bring it under explicit norms and to encourage both those inclined to evade interventions they ought to conduct and those inclined to launch interventions from which they ought to restrain themselves to worry at least more than they do now about what they could say before the court of world opinion.'[33] Other institutional solutions have been suggested by the International Commission on Intervention and State Sovereignty in its recent report, *The Responsibility to Protect*.[34]

Four rules of thumb

From the preceding synthesis, four rules of thumb can be distilled for evaluating the ethics of the Bush Administration's grand strategy. I use the term 'rules of thumb' deliberately, as my goal is to identify rough measures that can serve as starting points for evaluation, not laws that might be applied in a doctrinaire or unreflective fashion. It is important to treat these principles holistically, in the sense that a tick against one but not others would leave the Administration's strategy ethically deficient. The four rules of thumb are as follows:

1   *A grand strategy mounted by a predominant state would be ethically justifiable if it serves, in a self-conscious and demonstrable way, the realization of cosmopolitan values, principally the satisfaction of global basic rights.* An example of this would be if an American Administration were to embark on a concerted programme to use its economic, material and social resources to reshape the nature of world order to enhance the protection and satisfaction of rights to subsistence, security and liberty. If such a project promised genuine gains in these areas, and if there was consistency of purpose and practice over time, it would be difficult not to judge this programme of ethical merit. The same could not be said, however, for a similarly ambitious project conducted in the name of self-interest or the interests of a minority of powerful states, corporations or individuals.

2   *A grand strategy mounted by a predominant state would be ethically justifiable if it is prosecuted within the existing framework of international procedural and substantive rules and norms.* Even if an American Administration were to embark on the kind of cosmopolitan programme specified

above, it would have to pursue that programme through the existing institutional rules and procedures of international society in order to ensure its legitimacy, both ethically and politically. These rules include everything, from the principles of self-determination and non-intervention, to the laws of war; and the core procedures of international society range from norms of treaty law to the decision-making rules of the Security Council. As the preceding discussion indicates, these institutions have moral and practical value; they contribute to the realization of both international public goods, traditionally understood, and cosmopolitan values, even if those contributions are less than adequate. Pursuing a grand strategy through such institutions means acknowledging the principal procedural and substantive rules of international society, and accepting that the primary mode of innovation and change must be communicative.

3 *A grand strategy mounted by a predominant state would be ethically justifiable if it helps to provide international public goods, but, to be consistent with rules of thumb 1 and 2, these goods would have to be compatible with the satisfaction of basic human rights, and negotiated and pursued through established institutional processes.* When scholars list the international public goods provided by great powers or hegemons, they usually stress a stable balance of power, open international markets, freedom of the high seas, etc. Some of these are more enduring than others; at most points in international history a stable balance of power has been a recognized good, but this is less the case for open international markets. In other words, as international systems evolve, so too does the list of valued public goods. If a dominant state believes that an international order faces challenges of such a magnitude as to justify large-scale revision, it is legitimate to ask what new public goods, if any, are demanded by this new environment. It is also reasonable

to ask that these goods be framed with reference to the satisfaction of the basic human rights to subsistence, security and liberty. Most importantly, however, it is crucial that the spectrum of appropriate international public goods be negotiated through existing institutional processes of international society. In the end, this is the only way to ensure that the resulting sets of goods are social rather than particular goods, and that compromises between order and justice are the products of collective political deliberation, not unilateral opportunism.

4 *Actions by a predominant state that violate primary international rules to which that state is obligated would be ethically justifiable only to prevent a supreme humanitarian emergency.* Self-defence cannot provide a legitimate justification for law-breaking actions, as existing laws governing the use of force provide ample, if clearly delineated, scope for such defence. The requirements of international peace and security provide no better justification, as these are collective goods that the community of states has the right to address collectively through the auspices of the United Nations, however imperfect these might be. If these laws and processes are genuinely inadequate to the task, then the predominant state has an obligation under rule of thumb 2 to use its capacities to reform these through established institutional processes. Only when a people is faced with mass starvation, enslavement or massacre is law-breaking action justified, and only when such action is the only thing that can prevent such humanitarian emergencies.

The ethics of moralists

As noted in the introduction, moralists invite moral scrutiny, and none more so than the Bush Administration.

All politicians lace their rhetoric with claims of moral righteousness, and American leaders have developed this into something of an art form. Yet the Bush Administration and its neo-conservative acolytes have done this with renewed vigour and crusading fervour. As Bush told graduates at West Point, 'We are in a conflict between good and evil, and America will call evil by its name.'[35] The discourse of these 'moralists', as the popular press have dubbed them,[36] is a cocktail of moral claims and postures, four of which stand out. At the broadest of levels, they claim to be champions of 'freedom, democracy, and free enterprise', their triumvirate of universal values. At an equally broad level, they present America as the keeper of international order, the paramount international public good. 'America has, and intends to keep, military strengths beyond challenge,' Bush told the West Point graduates, 'thereby, making destabilizing arms races of other eras pointless, and limiting rivalries to trade and other pursuits to peace.'[37] These 'self-less' goals of freedom and order are bolstered by more self-interested, yet equally moral, claims. Appeals to the right of self-defence are prominent in the Administration's justification of its revisionist project. On the eve of war with Iraq, Bush told the American people that 'America's cause is right and just: liberty for an oppressed people, and security for the American people.'[38] The final moral posture adopted by the Administration is veiled and amorphous, yet nonetheless important. This is the posture of righteous victimhood, the idea that since America has suffered a grievous harm it has the right to avenge itself, a right that entitles Washington to considerable freedom of action.

At first glance, aspects of this moral cocktail appear to resonate with at least one or two of our rules of thumb. The values of freedom, democracy and free enterprise are related to the basic right of liberty, even if this relationship is less than straightforward; and international order is not unreasonably cast as an international public good. But this having been said, the dissonance between the Bush Doctrine and our ethical framework is more pronounced than its resonance.

With regard to the first of our rules of thumb – that a global hegemonic strategy should only be considered just if it contributes to the satisfaction of basic human rights – it is difficult to get beyond the patent contradictions in the Bush Administration's position. Let us take the right to liberty, for example. Championing this right features prominently in the Administration's rhetoric. 'By the resolve and purpose of America, and our friends and allies,' Bush told the American Enterprise Institute, 'we will make this an age of progress and liberty.'[39] It is well to remember, though, that Rousseau famously observed that 'Obedience to the law one has prescribed for oneself is liberty'.[40] Globally, this would have to mean two things, at the very minimum: that within states individuals or their representatives would have to be the legislators of national laws; and that internationally states, as imperfect representatives of their peoples, would have to be authors of international rules. Much of the Administration's talk about spreading democracy seems to relate to the first of these requirements, but this is contradicted by two things. The first is the absolutist nature of the Administration's crusade, with its categorical belief that there is but a single model of national success. How compatible is this absolutism with the fact that genuine liberty for the world's peoples would, of necessity, produce diversity, especially in a culturally heterogeneous global order? The second thing is the nature of the Administration's war against terrorism and rogue states. A prominent, though hidden, aspect of this war is dramatic empowerment of the CIA to wage covert operations globally, including the use of extra-judicial killing (as in Yemen). Even if the Administration engaged in a vigorous diplomatic push to enhance liberty globally, how successful could this be if it is simultaneously engaged in patently undemocratic forms of covert violence and subterfuge? If we turn to the requirement that internationally states should be the authors of international rules, the picture is not much brighter. We must simply ask here: is the Administration's unabashed unilateralism and barely disguised disdain for international institutions compatible with the community of states legislating the rules of international society?

This brings us to our second rule of thumb, that the prosecution of a hegemonic grand strategy ought to be institutionally governed. To meet this requirement, a preponderant state would need to acknowledge the principal procedural and substantive rules of international society. All of the evidence suggests that the Bush Administration treats such rules with disdain. Its penchant for bucking the rules is legendary. To name but a few of its law-disdaining actions: it has unsuccessfully tried to destroy the Kyoto Protocol and the International Criminal Court; it has withdrawn from the Anti-Ballistic Missile Treaty; it is the only country, other than Somalia, not to ratify the Optional Protocol on the Involvement of Children in Armed Conflict; it has scuttled efforts to strengthen the Biological Weapons Convention; it has worked to undermine the Chemical Weapons Convention; it shows no interest in ratifying the Comprehensive Test Ban Treaty; and it holds hundreds of prisoners at Guantanamo Bay in violation of at least fifteen articles of the Laws of War.[41] Its most flagrant violation of international law, however, is its decision to wage war on Iraq without Security Council endorsement, an action we examine in greater detail in the concluding chapter. Aside from its law-breaking aspects, this act also showed the Administration's attitude to the second dimension of this rule of thumb: accepting that the primary mode of innovation and change must be communicative. The Administration entered the Security Council process with an ultimatum: endorse the use of force or we will act unilaterally. Despite the fact that the majority of the Council preferred to use a combination of containment and a revitalized inspection regime, and despite the fact that the Administration seemed to lose diplomatic ground as the process unfolded, at no time would it accept any delay in its timetable for war. Throughout this process, senior Administration officials, perhaps with the exception of Colin Powell, showed little concern for the interests of other states, for building upon existing rules or for genuine negotiation. Overall, the Bush Administration's rule of thumb in this area appears to be that any international rules or procedures that complicate its freedom of action should be skirted, violated or undermined.

Our third rule of thumb holds that revisionist actions by a predominant state might be ethically justifiable if those actions help deliver international public goods, as long as those goods are compatible with the satisfaction of basic human rights and are negotiated through established institutional processes. The Bush Administration's rhetoric is replete with references to the international goods its grand strategy serves, but the paramount good appears to be the creation of 'a balance of power that favors human freedom'. As chapter 2 explained, this means two things. First, that Washington will vigorously defend American primacy, ensuring that no other great powers are able to challenge it for ascendancy, and that rogue states and terrorists cannot undermine national and international security. And, second, that such a 'balance' will facilitate the spread of the 'single sustainable model for national success: freedom, democracy, and free enterprise'. Although these ideas contain the conventional language of international public goods, such as the maintenance of the balance of power, and although some of the values this balance is meant to serve resonate with the cosmopolitan values advocated here, they still fall short of meeting this third rule of thumb.

To begin with, the onus is on American policy-makers to demonstrate that unbalanced American primacy is in fact an international public good. They must demonstrate that such primacy can actually deliver heightened global security and well-being, because anything less than this is likely to encourage international insecurity and competition from other powers. The Bush Administration's poor record in this respect was evident in the unprecedented global opposition to America's war in Iraq. Second, freedom and democracy, if not free enterprise, may well be desirable human goods, but we know that in 'really existing' human societies these values mean many different things, and that if they were propagated globally they would produce diverse forms of polity. The Bush Administration may be seriously committed to spreading these values, but America's track record over the past fifty years suggests that Washington may be seriously intolerant towards really existing democracies that do not serve American political, military or economic interests. Universalism and intolerance may well go hand in hand. Let us ask, for example, whether a genuine democracy in postwar Iraq – one that truly expresses Iraqi public opinion – is likely to be sympathetic to Washington's geo-strategic interests in the Middle East, and whether it will be tolerated if it is not. Third, as the previous paragraph noted, the Bush Administration is determined to prosecute its grand strategy outside established international institutions if necessary and, consistent with this, it has shown little inclination to engage in international dialogue about what might constitute the most pressing international public goods in need of sponsorship.

The final rule of thumb stipulates that actions by a predominant state that violate primary international rules to which that state is obligated would be ethically justifiable only to prevent a supreme humanitarian emergency. Two observations can be made here about the Bush Administration's doctrine and practice. First, the Administration has had no qualms about violating primary international rules to which the United States is formally obligated, either under treaty law or customary law. All of these violations were committed for reasons quite distinct from stemming humanitarian emergencies. The most noteworthy of these pertain to the laws of war, both *jus ad bellum* and *jus in bello*. Though controversial, the weight of international legal opinion holds that the war against Iraq, conducted without explicit Security Council endorsement, was a violation of Charter rules governing the exercise of force. With regard to laws governing the conduct of war once launched, actions like the imprisonment of suspected Taliban and al-Qaeda fighters at Guantanamo Bay violate multiple rules governing the treatment of prisoners of war, and may also violate the Constitution of the United States.[42] Second, the Administration has self-consciously employed the language of humanitarianism to justify actions motivated primarily by self-interest. Both the war in Afghanistan and in Iraq have been cast as humanitarian interventions to free subject peoples from tyrannical regimes that were guilty of the most heinous human rights violations. Nothing here suggests that these regimes were anything other than what they were accused of being, but several things cast doubt on the Administration's humanitarian credentials. Self-interested reasons loom large for both interventions; the Administration has befriended other tyrannies with terrible human rights records, such as Pakistan and Saudi Arabia; and the Administration has shown little interest in intervening in countries on the verge of genuine humanitarian emergencies, such as the Sudan, the Democratic Republic of Congo, or Zimbabwe. One might well ask whether the Bush Administration would be any more inclined to intervene in a contemporary Rwanda or Bosnia than its predecessors were, and its track record so far gives good cause for scepticism.

Conclusion

This chapter set out to answer a series of questions: what type of political project is the Bush Administration pursuing, and what is the international context in which it is prosecuting that project? What ethical principles would be appropriate for assessing the Administration's grand strategy, and how does it rate against those principles? The preceding discussion has portrayed the Bush Doctrine as a radical project of hegemonic renewal, being prosecuted in a global order marked by great complexity and challenges. After surveying five ethical positions for assessing the exercise of hegemonic power, I proposed a pragmatic synthesis of three of these, a synthesis tentatively termed 'procedural solidarism'. This position gives normative priority to the pursuit of cosmopolitan values, but prudential priority to the pursuit of such values through existing international institutional rules and processes, broadly defined. It thus seeks to strike a 'forward leaning' balance between the demands of justice and order. To 'operationalize' this balance I distilled four rules of thumb, which I then held up against the Administration's stated objectives. The result is not heartening. While the Bush team projects cosmopolitan-sounding goals, these are contradicted by other elements of their doctrine. While they express support for international institutions, their politics of ultimatum and exit belies this expression. And while they veil their interventions in humanitarian language, their record merely bolsters realist scepticism about the morality of great powers.

As we have seen in chapter 2, neo-conservatives place great emphasis on America's soft power, on its ability to achieve its objectives by winning the hearts and minds of the world's peoples. This is found in their constant references to the universality of American values, to the benign nature of American hegemony, and to the cultural magnetism of American society and institutions. There is, however, a crucial aspect of soft power that they neglect, largely because their view of power is non-social. A state can be said to have soft power when its social identity resonates with the principal norms of international society, which then gives its interests and actions a certain legitimacy. Other actors accept such a state's leadership because they see it as the embodiment of prevailing international social norms. No state is, of course, the perfect embodiment of such norms, nor do states consistently live out their social identities. But a liberal state that acts illiberally with respect to liberal cosmopolitan norms and the core procedural rules of international society is in serious risk of undermining its soft power. Being, and being seen to be, ethically legitimate is not only critically important for global order, therefore, but also for the future of America's global political influence.

5

Coercion and Exit

As the US-led war on Iraq unfolded, Charles Krauthammer published an ever-confident restatement of his
unipolar moment thesis. The course of world events, he
argues, has merely vindicated his original claims. 'Contrary to expectation, the United States has not regressed
to the mean; rather, its dominance has dramatically increased.'[1] Unlike hegemons of the past, the United States
'is dominant by every measure: military, economic, technological, diplomatic, cultural, even linguistic, with a
myriad of countries trying to fend off the inexorable
march of Internet-fueled MTV English'.[2] This fact of
unipolarity gives the United States the unique possibility
of pursuing a 'new unilateralist' foreign policy, one that
sees American interests extending well beyond self-
defence, to include the pursuit of a balance of power that
favours freedom. This involves two global interests:
'extending the peace by advancing democracy and pre-
serving the peace by acting as balancer of last resort'.[3]

As before, Krauthammer ridicules those who stress the
importance of the United Nations and multilateralism. He
decries the idea that the United Nations Security Council
could or should determine the legitimacy of American
actions, particularly those involving the use of force. 'The
Security Council is, on the very rare occasions when it

actually works, realpolitik by committee. But by what logic is it a repository of international morality?'[4] He condemns those who want to see 'the multilateral handcuffing of American power', arguing that the United States must define its interests and assemble fluid coalitions of the willing to help prosecute those interests. 'Coalitions are not made by superpowers going begging hat in hand. They are made by asserting a position and inviting others to join.'[5] If others are unwilling, then the United States must be prepared to act alone or with whoever will follow. Although he wrote his restatement before the Security Council's deliberations on Iraq had foundered, he anticipated precisely the Bush Administration's strategy. 'No unilateralist would, say, reject Security Council support for an attack on Iraq. The nontrivial question that separates unilateralism from multilateralism . . . is this: What do you do if, at the end of the day the Security Council refuses to back you? Do you allow yourself to be dictated to on issues of vital national – and international – security?'[6]

The preceding chapters suggest that ideas such as these are mistaken to the point of being dangerous. They are, in the first instance, patently idealistic, even utopian. Not in the inter-war sense of idealism, as having a misguided faith in the power of human reason or peace through law, but in the sense of having an unqualified faith in America's transformative capacities, in the sense of imagining American interests as universal, in the sense of denying that other members of international society might have legitimate differences about the future of world order, and in the sense of ignoring the very real cultural diversity and agency of the world's peoples. All of this amounts to a grand denial of the ubiquity of politics, the essence of idealism. More than this, though, the theory of power that underlies the Bush Doctrine is marred by a series of profound flaws. It assumes that there is a simple causal relationship between power resources and political influence, but America's frustrated diplomacy suggests that this relationship is at best attenuated. A conception of power that focuses just on resources will thus be a poor guide to effective national policy, as it neglects, by definition, the other ingredients of influence.

The second flaw is the assumption that American practices are legitimate because American interests are expressed as being universal, not because they are endorsed by the international community. All this does is blind American policy-makers to the very real international politics of legitimacy, which they can choose not to see but cannot wish away. The third flaw is the assumption of American cultural magnetism. Even if large sectors of the world's population covet American cultural artefacts, this does not mean that they view American foreign policy uncritically or are incapable of giving those artefacts new meanings and purposes – meanings and purposes not necessarily compatible with American interests.

These conceptual or theoretical flaws are compounded by the misfit between the Bush Administration's understanding of power and the reality of contemporary global structures and processes. For all of the Administration's romantic analogizing of the world today with that after the Second World War, the two worlds are radically different. States such as Britain, Germany and France are no longer existentially dependent on the United States, and they also lack a strong perception of a common threat. Their economic dependence on the United States has given way to economic interdependence, and international economic relations are now heavily structured by institutional rules and processes. The density of international institutions has increased dramatically, international society has become ever more embedded in world society and normative agency has been widely diffused. This new world is unlikely to be amenable to simplistic power projection policies, and a project of hegemonic renewal that neglects the need for legitimacy and institutionally embedded authority should not be expected to serve America's medium- to long-term interests. They will not be encouraged in this respect if the Bush Administration's grand strategy and the practices it engenders are judged unethical. Chapter 4 offered one framework for assessing this, which I tentatively termed procedural solidarism. Interestingly, it is not the fact that this framework gives normative priority to the pursuit of cosmopolitan values that makes the Bush strategy look bad; the Administration's rhetorical emphasis on liberty and freedom is not entirely out of order, even though its contradictory practices are. The rule of thumb that stands at odds with the Administration's strategy is the requirement that change be institutionally governed, something that clearly conflicts with its 'new unilateralism'. It is this amalgam of universalist rhetoric and law-breaking unilateralism that will leave many around the world judging American policies to be both unjust and illegitimate.

This concluding chapter explores, in a preliminary fashion, the implications of the above argument for the future of American diplomacy and global order. There is no doubt that an American Administration that believes effective influence develops from unipolarity and unilateralism – and one that commands the military and economic resources of the United States – has the ability to thrust issues on to the international agenda and to impose its will on those who are vulnerable to force or bribery. But, as the first part of this chapter explains, it must work with a radically circumscribed repertoire of diplomatic techniques, most notably coercion and exit. In the highly complex global order described in chapter 3, these techniques are at best sub-optimal and at worst self-defeating. They can deliver regime change in Iraq, but they cannot deliver social legitimacy, and if they remain the modus operandi of American foreign policy they risk undercutting American soft power and generating multiple forms of global resistance, neither of which is desirable for the medium- to long-term protection of America's global interests. I illustrate the costs of such Procrustean diplomacy through a necessarily brief examination of the Administration's diplomatic defeat in the Security Council over war with Iraq. The second and final part of the chapter examines the implications for global order if the Administration's approach to American foreign policy persists. I highlight four potential consequences: the increased frequency of 'institutional balancing' in international relations, the growing disenchantment and activism of diverse actors in global civil society, the tendency for other states to engage in various forms of geo-strategic balancing, and the continued failure to address the 'triad of disorder'.

American diplomacy

Neo-conservative policy-makers and commentators see unilateralism alloyed to unipolarity as liberating, enabling the United States to shake off the shackles of both misguided isolationism and internationalism in order to finally realize its national and global interests. But their view of power in general, American power in particular, and the unilateralist posture they advocate might instead form an iron cage, a set of self-imposed constraints on America's diplomatic repertoire. If we define diplomacy broadly, to include a spectrum of techniques that states employ to further their objectives in international relations, then it would include everything from outright military coercion to artful persuasion. Between these extremes it would include a variety of techniques, including bribery, the threat or practice of exiting from institutions of cooperation, explanation and negotiation. It is commonsensical, I believe, that states seeking maximum influence would wish to master, and be able to deploy, as many of these techniques as possible. This is even more likely to be the case in highly complex global orders marked by extensive interdependence, dense institutionalization and diffuse normative agency. In such orders, techniques that approach the coercive end of the spectrum are likely to be of declining utility, a point borne out by the extensive literature on the reduced fungibility of military power under conditions of high interdependence. We now live in just such a highly complex global order, but instead of augmenting America's diplomatic repertoire, neo-conservatives in the Bush Administration have radically circumscribed it. If one views power as possessive, primarily material, subjective and non-social, if one believes that one is endowed with unrivalled power so defined, and if one decides that the best way to exploit this power is unilaterally, then coercion, bribery and exit will be your preferred repertoire of techniques, and the more social, communicative forms of diplomacy, such as explanation, negotiation or persuasion, will be neglected.

Not surprisingly, coercion and exit, in particular, have featured prominently in the Administration's engagement with the world. Its willingness to threaten and apply military force to achieve its objectives is most palpable in its campaign against 'axis of evil' states, but it is also apparent in its dictum that 'you're either with us or against us' in the war against terrorism and rogue states – an assertion that effectively places dissenters in the same category as enemies. As we have seen in chapter 2, the threat and practice of exiting from institutions of international cooperation has become the Administration's favoured mode of institutional politics: if it wants other parties to bend to its will, it threatens to leave; if they don't yield, or if the Administration is sufficiently disenchanted with the regime in question, it removes the United States from the framework of cooperation. In doing so, it brings to the fore a deep tendency in American political culture. As Albert Hirschman famously argued, the 'preference for the neatness of exit over the messiness and heartbreak of voice has then "persisted throughout our national history"'.[7]

America's historic defeat in the United Nations Security Council over war with Iraq illustrates the diplomatic modus operandi of the Bush Administration, as well as the limits of its approach. The magnitude of the defeat was evident in the response of leading American newspapers, once it became clear that the United States had failed to gain the requisite nine votes for a new resolution authorizing the use of force. As Steven Weisman wrote in *The New York Times*, 'Just about everyone involved now acknowledges that a train of miscalculations and misunderstandings has produced a setback for American diplomacy and world standing.'[8] That a major setback occurred is without doubt, but the loss was ultimately due to Washington's diplomatic strategy more than miscalculation and misunderstanding. As noted in chapter 1, removing Saddam Hussein from power was one of the causes célèbres of the Project for a New American Century. In 1998, Paul Wolfowitz told the House of Representatives National Security Committee that the Clinton Administration was 'unwilling to pursue a serious policy in Iraq, one that would aim at liberating the Iraqi people from Saddam's tyrannical grasp and free Iraq's neighbors from Saddam's murderous threats'.[9] Soon after assuming office, Donald Rumsfeld's Pentagon started developing military options for Iraq, and we now know that immediately after the

September 11 attacks Rumsfeld and Wolfowitz tried to convince the President and the National Security Council to 'go against Iraq, not just Al Qaeda'.[10] Bush was ultimately persuaded, however, to defer dealing with Iraq until after the war in Afghanistan was completed, but nobody on the Council doubted the need to go after Saddam in the near future.

Had majority opinion prevailed in the Administration, the United States would never have returned to the Security Council for a new resolution supporting military action against Iraq. By early September 2002, however, it was clear that a renewed burst of United Nations diplomacy would be needed to gain bipartisan support in Congress and international support from other major powers. The Administration's subsequent strategy is a case study in the diplomacy of coercion and exit. The other members of the Security Council were given an ultimatum – endorse the use of force to disarm and (indirectly) dethrone Saddam, or follow the League of Nations into the dustbin of history. 'All the world now faces a test,' Bush told the United Nations General Assembly, 'and the United Nations a difficult and defining moment. Are Security Council resolutions to be honored and enforced, or cast aside without consequence? Will the United Nations serve the purpose of its founding, or will it be irrelevant?'[11] This ultimatum was backed up by the coercive threat of exit. If the Security Council was not willing to endorse military action, the United States would act alone or with a coalition of the willing. In Bush's words, 'We will work with the U.N. Security Council for the necessary resolutions. But the purposes of the United States should not be doubted. The Security Council resolutions will be enforced . . . or action will be unavoidable.'[12]

Once the Administration had re-entered the Security Council process, though, its understanding and practice of power was dysfunctional to say the least. The institutional rules and processes of the Security Council changed the nature of politics. By virtue of these rules, the Council's other fourteen members were empowered with votes, and four others had the power of veto. In such a world, the threat or use of force to obtain compliance is illegitimate – it may still occur, but must be hidden, never spoken publicly, and is likely to be of little utility with the major veto states. In such an institutionally structured world, the diplomacy of explanation, negotiation and persuasion is at a premium. Yet this is precisely what the Administration's diplomacy of coercion and exit could not accommodate.

Immediately after Bush's speech to the United Nations, expressions of support came from many states, including France and Germany. And within a week Iraq had volunteered to allow UN weapons inspection teams to return 'without conditions'. It soon became clear, however, that Council members were divided over how best to proceed. The Administration was frustrated by Iraq's decision, as it had long held that inspections simply allowed Saddam to continue his game of cat and mouse with the international community. Others, particularly the French, saw hope for a newly invigorated sanctions regime and the possibility of disarming and containing Iraq without war.[13] Behind this difference lay conflicts of national self-interest, but also, and perhaps more importantly, profound disagreements over the management of international peace and security. As we have seen, the Administration believed that only the unwavering application of American power could ensure national security and global order. The Europeans, on the other hand, were deeply suspicious of the Bush Doctrine, and their experience of regional peace through institutions made them more inclined to uphold international rules and processes.

These differences underlay two months of intensive 'ne-gotiation' on the Security Council, which ultimately pro-duced Resolution 1441 on 8 November 2002. The Administration was able to claim victory because it had secured a new Security Council ultimatum for Iraq, sup-ported by all fifteen Council members. But Resolution 1441 was, if anything, a victory for French diplomacy. The French had vigorously opposed any resolution that would give the United States the right to use force, and argued instead for an initial resolution that would set down clear disarmament requirements for Iraq and re-establish an invigorated inspections regime. If Iraq failed to comply, the Security Council would have to meet again to pass a second resolution. In essence, this is what 1441 did. It gave Iraq 'a final opportunity to comply with its disarma-ment requirements', mandated that inspectors be given 'unimpeded, unconditional, and unrestricted access', de-cided that the Council would 'convene immediately' to consider any breaches by Iraq, and also warned that it would 'face serious consequences' if it did not comply.[14]

The Bush Administration had insisted that the Security Council stand firm and authorize the use of force. Instead Resolution 1441 put two obstacles in front of such author-ization: it sent the inspectors back into Iraq, and made further Security Council action dependent upon their judgements about Iraqi compliance; it also encouraged the view that a second resolution would be needed to license the use of force. The Administration immediately bucked against both of these constraints. No sooner had the inspectors returned to Iraq than the Administration started insisting that Iraq was in 'material breach', and it vigorously denied that another resolution would be needed to sanction war. Resolutions 678, 687 and 1441 all pro-vided such sanction, it claimed. This was not the view, however, of the majority of the Security Council. Most wanted the inspectors to be given time to complete comprehensive investigations and assessments, and most believed that war would be illegal without another resolution. Added to this, America's principal ally – the British Prime Minister Tony Blair – was facing a parliamentary revolt and unprecedented levels of public opposition to war.

By January 2003, increasingly acrimonious divisions had emerged between the United States and Britain, on the one hand, and France, Germany and Russia, on the other. The deployment of a massive invasion force was already well under way, and it was clear that Washington was determined to launch a war by March at the latest, with or without UN support. Eventually the Administration agreed to seek support for another resolution, and the US and Britain tabled their preferred draft in late February. This was not, however, a sign that Washington was prepared to compromise or modify its timetable for war. The draft resolution simply endorsed 1441 and declared that Iraq was in material breach; no attempt was made to accommodate the interests of other member states in allowing the inspectors to complete their work. By this time over 10 million people around the world had protested against war, and France and Russia had both indicated a willingness to veto any new resolution that licensed war before the inspectors were done. Rather than compromise, the Administration engaged in frenetic lobbying to gain what Blair called a 'moral majority' – a majority of nine Council votes, even if France or Russia then vetoed. All this time the Administration maintained the threat of exit, and reports indicate that it placed intense pressure on the weaker, non-permanent members of the Council. There were two situations in which the United States was willing to put its draft resolution to a vote: if it thought it could win; or if it thought it would get a moral majority, but then have the resolution vetoed by one of the permanent members. In early March, Bush was insisting that it would be put to a vote, and that Council members would be forced to show their cards. In the end, though, it was clear that the Administration's diplomacy of coercion and exit had failed to secure Council support, and that if the resolution was put to a vote it would fail to gain the moral majority. On 17 March it withdrew the resolution from the table and exited to war.

Three observations can be made about this story. First, the Administration only entered the Security Council processes because seeking United Nations endorsement was necessary to secure Congressional and international support, a point impressed on Bush by his Secretary of State, Colin Powell, and his closest ally, Tony Blair. Working through the institutional processes of the UN was thus a test of the legitimacy of the Administration's plans. Second, once enmeshed in the Security Council processes, the Administration adopted a diplomatic stance completely ill-suited to gaining Council endorsement. The strategy of coercion and exit seems to have been completely counter-productive – non-permanent members resented being bullied and not having their concerns addressed, and France, Germany and Russia began to see containing the United States as important as disarming Saddam. At no point did the Administration display any interest in compromising or negotiating, even though the evidence suggests that if it had been willing to delay the onset of war until the inspectors had completed their work then they may well have gained a resolution licensing the use of force. Finally, the Administration's failure to gain Council endorsement for war meant that the ensuing conflict was immediately judged illegal and illegitimate by large sectors of global society. The vicissitudes of legitimacy and reputation are difficult to quantify, but one would need to be an optimist to believe that diplomatic misadventures such as this are not subversive of the soft power American policy-makers so cherish.

Some may argue that Washington's failure to gain Security Council endorsement has ultimately been inconsequential – the Bush Administration wanted Saddam deposed, it was willing to act alone if necessary, and when the international community failed to match its words with deeds America's military might was deployed with devastating effect. What this misses, though, is the way in which the Security Council's refusal to legitimate the war has greatly increased the costs of failure for the Administration. If the Council had sanctioned the use of force, Washington could have socialized these costs, arguing that even though the mission failed to achieve one or more of its core objectives it had been a collective decision to proceed, based on a joint assessment of the ends to be achieved and the likelihood of success. Without Council endorsement, the Administration can afford nothing less than total success, as it alone must bear the full costs of failure. The risks of this were evident during the second week of the war, when stronger than anticipated Iraqi resistance exposed the Administration to sustained criticism, even ridicule. The subsequent military victory provided short-term relief from criticism, but since then the Administration has faced test after test of its credibility. To measure up to its pre-war rhetoric, the Administration has needed Iraqis dancing in the streets, Saddam's arsenal of chemical, biological and nuclear weapons found, peace and stability in Iraq established, recognizable democratic institutions and processes quickly constructed, the incidence of terrorism reduced, and the war to yield some identifiable peace dividend in the Middle East. Prior to war, critics questioned Washington's ability to deliver these goods, and, having acted outside the United Nations and the framework of international law, it can be expected that high reputational, as well as material, costs will be imposed on the Administration if these goods are not forthcoming.

Global order

When a state with the material preponderance of the United States embarks on a revisionist project of hegemonic renewal, global order cannot but be affected. This is especially so when revisionism extends to the neglectful corrosion or wilful subversion of established institutions of international governance. Some commentators have anticipated the death or paralysis of the United Nations, together with a general weakening of international cooperation. My own view is that the impact is likely to be complex and variegated, and will be determined as much by the agency and interests of other states and non-state actors as it will by crash-through-or-crash politics of the Administration. A detailed study of the impact on a highly institutionalized global order of superpower revisionism is a project for another book, but I wish to sketch here several likely consequences of the Bush Administration's grand strategy.

The first of these is the increased frequency of institutional balancing in international relations. The Administration is probably correct that other great powers will not have the capabilities to balance the United States militarily or economically for several decades. But this does not mean that these states will not explore other means to corral and tame the United States and to carve out realms of individual or collective autonomy. The most likely of these means is institutional. Under conditions of high interdependence, cooperation and coordination problems abound, and institutions remain the most effective means that states have yet developed to address these problems. Despite the Bush Administration's repeated attempts to sideline or destroy a range of international institutions, other states remain strongly committed to institutional governance, both normatively and pragmatically. Institutions are also levellers; they embed politics within rule-governed roles and processes.

States are likely, therefore, to try to defend and extend the architecture of institutional governance through at least three practices. First, they can be expected to resist subversive American institutional practices, raising the general level of contestation within existing institutions. Second, they are likely to resort increasingly to a strategy of institution jumping. That is, to extending their institutional conflicts with Washington from one regime to another. France and Germany did this during the Security Council contest over Iraq. At the high point of the contest they extended their campaign to the forum of NATO, where they tried to frustrate American war plans by threatening to deny Turkey alliance protection if it agreed to station American troops on its soil. Finally, they can be expected to engage in increased extra-American institution building. When states are committed to furthering cooperation in a particular issue-area but are faced with American intransigence or opposition, one option will be to go ahead and create the institution they want but without American participation. At times, the costs of such actions will seem too high, but states are already taking this route with increasing frequency. The creation of the International Criminal Court is a case in point, as is the Kyoto Protocol. It looks likely as well that Washington's wavering on participation in the renegotiation of the 1988 Basle Capital Adequacy accord will see European states proceed on their own, with potentially serious costs for American banks operating in Europe.

A second consequence is likely to be growing global disenchantment and activism among diverse non-state actors. The Bush Administration's understanding of power in international relations neither acknowledges nor accommodates the politics of such actors, and yet one of the consequences of its policies may well be the provocation and aggravation of such groups. If American unilateralism can be expected to increase inter-state tensions, even among traditional allies, then in an international society deeply embedded in world society one can expect that disaffection to encompass civil-society actors. It is unlikely, however, that disenchantment will take one form or mode. At the most general level, unease has already spread among the citizenry of the world's major democracies. It is only with reference to such unease that we can explain why 10 million people took to the streets to protest against war with Iraq – the prospect of a unilateral American war became a lightning rod for concern about the direction of American foreign policy after September 11. At another level, American unilateralism is likely to increase opposition to economic globalization. Even if this unilateralism is not manifest in the more aggressive prosecution of Washington's global economic agenda – which appears unlikely – American self-interest unmasked will almost certainly stimulate greater opposition than when it is obscured by purported or genuine multilateralism. Finally, it is difficult to see how the Bush Administration's militant unilateralism will not generate more anti-systemic violence from disaffected extremists. Despite its rhetoric to the contrary, it is possible that the Administration is doing nothing more than overlaying the global mosaic of failed or unresponsive political institutions and chronic maldistribution of wealth with a heightened structure of domination. When we look at the failure of states such as Britain in Northern Ireland, Spain in the Basque region and India in Kashmir to crush violent anti-systemic movements through force, it seems unlikely that domination applied globally can bring American or global security. More than this, though, heightened domination can be expected to breed heightened violent resistance, of which the attacks on Riyadh and Morocco may be harbingers.

In addition to stimulating institutional balancing and heightened unease and resistance in global civil society, realists are probably correct that the Bush Doctrine is likely to provoke geo-strategic balancing as well. As noted on pages 150–1, the prospect of a state seriously challenging America's military might is minimal over the next decade or so. This having been said, though, three types of balancing behaviour should be expected. First of all, there is likely to be 'balancing for autonomy', in which regional groupings develop or augment their collective military capabilities to reduce their dependence on the United States for regional security. The only grouping with an ability to do this in the short-term is the European Union, but if the Bush Administration's militant unilateralism persists we can expect the EU to move forward with current plans for a rapid deployment force with added commitment. Second, a growing number of states are likely to engage in the exceedingly dangerous practice of 'threshold balancing'. There is little doubt that the Administration's stance has given some states the message that the only way to guarantee regime security is to seek a rudimentary nuclear capacity. Ironically, Washington's campaign against rogue states with weapons of mass destruction – based on at best questionable intelligence – may increase the incentives for some regimes to move ever so stealthily towards the nuclear threshold. The Administration's flagrant disregard for its own disarmament obligations under the Nuclear Non-Proliferation

Treaty, and its exit from core arms control institutions such as the Anti-Ballistic Missile Treaty, have only added to this problem, as they reduce confidence in the non-proliferation regime and they give other states a sense that the global arms control compact has been fractured. Finally, as the Administration's militant unilateralism erodes America's image as a benign hegemon, other states may well start to see it as a potential threat. States such as China are unlikely to respond in a dramatic or provocative fashion, but a risk of the Bush Doctrine is that it will encourage them to plot a new long-term course, one that will involve augmenting their long-term capacities to meet, if not match, the United States militarily.

Finally, the above consequences will probably make it more rather than less difficult for the international community to address, in any serious and effective manner, the triad of disorder. Reducing the domestication of violence, alleviating the persistent maldistribution of global wealth and protecting the global environment are all profound collective action problems. They are global in nature and effect, and they cannot be addressed unilaterally. Reducing the domestication of violence requires creating new institutional mechanisms, both within states and internationally, that will permit legal reform and change. It also requires deep multilateral policing and intelligence networks that can effectively constrain national, regional and global terrorism, while furthering the development of democratic institutions – a difficult task indeed. Alleviating the persistent maldistribution of global wealth requires not just the opening up of global markets, but the wholesale reform of the global terms of trade. It also requires greatly augmented, if better targeted and deployed, foreign aid. The Bush Administration has, to its credit, doubled the dollar amount of American aid, but the general orientation of its unilateralist foreign policy, in stimulating the above-cited consequences, is undermining the conditions of global order that are necessary for a concerted multilateral response to profound global poverty. Stemming the global environmental crisis requires not just comprehensive global cooperation across a wide range of environmental issues, but also serious reductions in civil conflict and chronic poverty. If the Bush Doctrine affects global order in the ways suggested above, the hurdles that must be cleared to achieve these objectives are likely to increase in number and scale.

Spectres of Rome and Athens

When George W. Bush addressed the United Nations General Assembly on the need for military action against Iraq, he said that 'a regime that has lost its legitimacy will also lose its power'.[15] The Iraqi regime had repeatedly violated Security Council resolutions and thus forfeited its right to the protections afforded by sovereignty. The implication was that legitimacy is tied to the observance of international rules and the authority of international institutions, and that power is dependent on institutionally governed legitimacy. One might well ask why the Bush Administration comprehends the importance of international legitimacy for Iraqi power, but fails to understand its importance with respect to American power. The international community is unlikely ever to challenge the sovereignty of the United States, but perceptions of illegitimacy, stimulated by disregard for international norms and institutional processes, can lead to more subtle yet significant erosions of power and political influence. The politics of coercion and exit stimulates such illegitimacy, and frustrated diplomacy is the first consequence. Adopting a crash-through-or-crash approach to this can only exacerbate the problem and further undermine America's ability to realize its national and global objectives. It is also bad news for global governance. The socially adroit exercise of American power can make a vital contribution to dealing with the challenges of the contemporary global order, but the narcissistic application of American might can only complicate these challenges.

It is well to recall here the decline of the Roman Empire and the collapse of Athenian power. We are constantly told that the United States is the greatest power since the days of Rome, an analogy that is meant to impress on us the sheer magnitude of American power; its only historical analogue being an empire most of us know only through epic Hollywood imagery. The analogy is more illuminating, however, when it comes to the sources of political decline. For Edward Gibbon, the great historian of the Roman Empire, it was the hubris of material power that sowed the seeds of decline. He wrote that the 'rise of a city which swelled into an empire may deserve, as a singular prodigy, the reflection of a philosophic mind. But the decline of Rome was the natural and inevitable effect of *immoderate greatness*.'[16] Thucydides, the historian of the Peloponnesian War, conveyed a similar message about the decline of Athenian power. On the eve of the war, Pericles cautioned the Athenians to wage a just war, and 'not to add to the empire while the war is in progess, and not to go out of your way to involve yourselves in new perils'.[17] As the war proceeded, the Athenians forgot Pericles' admonition and lost sight of the moral bases of their power. Intoxicated by their own might, they eventually launched an ambitious invasion of Sicily. They 'were utterly and entirely defeated; their sufferings were on an enormous scale; their losses were . . . total; army, navy, everything was destroyed, and out of many, only a few returned'.[18] Historical analogies must always be treated with great care – as the Bush Administration's romance with the immediate post-1945 period indicates. Yet both Gibbon and Thucydides draw our attention to the dangers of hubris, and one might well ask whether the idealism of preponderance currently ascendant in Washington will have the same detrimental effects as Rome's 'immoderate greatness'.

Notes

Introduction

1   Kenneth N. Waltz, 'The continuity of international politics', in *Worlds in Collision: Terror and the Future of Global Order*, eds Ken Booth and Tim Dunne (London: Palgrave Macmillan, 2002), pp. 348–53, at p. 350.

2   Stephen G. Brooks and William Wohlforth, 'American primacy in perspective', *Foreign Affairs*, 81, 4 (2002), pp. 20–33, at pp. 30–1.

3   The Bush Administration has recently embarked on a vigorous campaign to strike so-called 'Article 98 Agreements' with other states, the effect of which is to give American forces immunity from prosecution under the International Criminal Court. The Administration's success in negotiating such agreements has been mixed, though. At the time of writing, no major European power has signed, and America's closest allies have either declined to sign or remain reluctant and undecided. The European Union has established guidelines for such agreements that maintain the integrity of the Court, and it is threatening that admission to the Union will be conditional upon states adhering to these guidelines. The Administration has had most success in striking agreements with states that are distant from Europe and materially weak, and thus vulnerable to the considerable pressure it is bringing to bear. This pressure includes the congressionally

mandated withdrawal of military aid. It is worth noting, however, that even with such pressure most states that have signed Article 98 agreements are not members of the Court. For a comprehensive study of these agreements, see: <http://www.humanrightswatch.org/campaigns/icc/docs/bilateralagreements.pdf>.

4 Hans H. Gerth and C. Wright Mills (eds), *From Max Weber: Essays in Sociology* (London: Routledge & Kegan Paul, 1948), p. 280.

5 Robert O. Keohane and Joseph S. Nye, *Power and Interdependence* (Boston, MASS: Little, Brown, 1977), p. 44.

Chapter 1 The Idealism of Preponderance

1 John Lewis Gaddis, *The Long Peace: Inquiries into the History of the Cold War* (Oxford: Oxford University Press, 1987); Kenneth Waltz, *Theory of International Politics* (New York: Random House, 1979), p. 180; and Kenneth Waltz, 'The stability of the bipolar world', *Daedalus*, 93, 3 (1964), pp. 881–909, at p. 899.

2 John Lewis Gaddis, 'A grand strategy of transformation', *Foreign Policy*, 133, November/December (2002), pp. 50–7, at p. 56.

3 Robert O. Keohane, *After Hegemony: Cooperation and Discord in the World Political Economy* (Princeton: Princeton University Press, 1984); and Keohane, *International Institutions and State Power: Essays in International Relations Theory* (Boulder, CO: Westview Press, 1989).

4 Robert Gilpin, *War and Change in World Politics* (Cambridge: Cambridge University Press, 1981).

5 Waltz, *Theory of International Politics*.

6 Gilpin, *War and Change*, p. 42.

7 Ibid., p. 43.

8 Ibid., p. 235.

9 See, for example, Richard Lugar, 'The republican course', *Foreign Policy*, 86, spring (1992), pp. 86–98.

10 Daniel Deudney and John Ikenberry, 'Who won the Cold War?', *Foreign Policy*, 87, summer (1992), pp. 123–38, at p. 125.
11 See William C. Wohlforth, 'Realism and the end of the Cold War', *International Security*, 19, 3, winter (1994/95), pp. 91–129.
12 Jeffrey Legro and Andrew Moravcsik, 'Is anybody still a realist?', *International Security*, 24, 2, fall (1999), pp. 5–55.
13 Ferenc Feher, 'Eastern Europe in the eighties', *Telos*, 45, fall (1980), pp. 5–18, at p. 14.
14 Edward P. Thompson, *Beyond the Cold War* (London: Merlin, 1982), pp. 32–3.
15 Christian Reus-Smit, 'Realist and resistance utopias: security and political action in the new Europe', *Millennium: Journal of International Studies*, 21, 1, spring (1992), pp. 1–28.
16 Greg Fry and Jacinta O'Hagan (eds), *Contending Images of World Politics* (London: Macmillan, 2000), pp. 2–3.
17 Richard Ned Lebow and Janice Gross Stein, *We All Lost the Cold War* (Princeton: Princeton University Press, 1994).
18 Charles Krauthammer, 'The unipolar moment', *Foreign Affairs*, 70, 1 (1990/91), pp. 23–33, at p. 24.
19 Ibid.
20 Ibid., p. 25.
21 Ibid., p. 33.
22 Francis Fukuyama, 'The end of history', *The National Interest*, 16, summer (1989), pp. 3–18.
23 Francis Fukuyama, *The End of History and the Last Man* (New York: Free Press, 1992), p. xi.
24 Ibid., pp. xi–xxiii.
25 Ibid., pp. 276–84.
26 For an early statement, see Michael Doyle, 'Kant, liberal legacies, and foreign affairs I', *Philosophy and Public Affairs*, 12, 3, summer (1983), pp. 205–35; and 'Kant, liberal legacies, and foreign affairs II', *Philosophy and Public Affairs*, 12, 4, fall (1983), pp. 323–53. See also Bruce Russett, *Grasping the Democratic Peace: Principles for a Post-Cold War World* (Princeton: Princeton University Press, 1993).

27 President Bill Clinton, 'State of the Union Address, 1994'. On the role that the promotion of democracy has played in American foreign policy historically, see Tony Smith, *America's Mission* (Princeton: Princeton University Press, 1994).

28 Larry Diamond, 'Promoting democracy', *Foreign Policy*, 87, summer (1992), pp. 25–46, at p. 26.

29 Ibid., p. 27.

30 The classic statement of this position was Paul Kennedy's book, *The Rise and Fall of the Great Powers: Economic Change and Military Conflict from 1500 to 2000* (New York: Random House, 1987).

31 Joseph S. Nye, 'Soft power', *Foreign Policy*, 80, fall (1990), pp. 153–71, at p. 168. See also Joseph S. Nye, *Bound to Lead* (New York: Basic Books, 1990).

32 Nye, 'Soft power', p. 171.

33 Kenneth Waltz, 'The new world order', *Millennium: Journal of International Studies*, 22, 2 (1993), pp. 187–95, at p. 190.

34 Christopher Layne, 'The unipolar illusion: why new great powers will rise', *International Security*, 17, 4 (1993), pp. 5–51.

35 John Mearsheimer, 'Back to the future: instability in Europe after the Cold War', *International Security*, 15, 1 (1990), pp. 5–56.

36 John Zysman, 'US power, trade, and technology', *International Affairs*, 67, 1 (1991), pp. 81–106.

37 Harris Wofford, 'The democratic challenge', *Foreign Policy*, 86, spring (1992), pp. 99–113, at p. 100.

38 Zysman, 'US power, trade, and technology', p. 103.

39 Samuel P. Huntington, 'Why international primacy matters', *International Security*, 17, 4, spring (1993), pp. 68–83, at p. 75.

40 Samuel P. Huntington, *The Clash of Civilizations and the Remaking of World Order* (London: Touchstone, 1996), p. 29.

41 Ibid., p. 21.

42 Ibid., p. 28.

43 Ibid., p. 29.

44 Henry Kissinger, *Diplomacy* (New York: Touchstone, 1994).

45 Robert Kaplan, 'The coming anarchy', *Atlantic Monthly*, 273, 2, February (1994); and Daniel Patrick Moynihan, *Pandaemonium: Ethnicity in International Politics* (Oxford: Oxford University Press, 1993).

46 Terry L. Deibel, 'Bush's foreign policy: mastery and inaction', *Foreign Policy*, 84, fall (1991), pp. 3–23, at p. 22.

47 See Andrew J. Bacevich, *American Empire: The Realities and Consequences of US Diplomacy* (Cambridge, MASS: Harvard University Press, 2002).

48 Quoted in R. W. Harris, *Absolutism and Enlightenment: 1660–1789* (London: Blandford Press, 1967), p. 76.

49 Quoted in Heather Neilson, 'Big words: issues of American self-representation', *Australasian Journal of American Studies*, 17, 1 (1998), pp. 3–21, at p. 3.

50 Democratic Representatives scored on average only 19.3 per cent, with many scoring zero. William Martin, 'The Christian right and American foreign policy', *Foreign Policy*, 114, spring (1999), pp. 66–80, at p. 70.

51 Project for the New American Century, 'Statement of principles', 3 June 1997: <http://www.newamericancentury.org/statementofprinciples.htm>.

52 Robert Kagan and William Kristol, 'The present danger', *The National Interest*, 59, spring (2000), pp. 57–69, at p. 58.

53 Zalmay Khalilzad, 'Losing the moment? The United States and the world after the Cold War', *Washington Quarterly*, 18, 2 (1995), pp. 87–107, at p. 94.

54 Ibid., pp. 95–103.

55 Kagan and Kristol, 'The present danger', pp. 65–6. Also see Project for the New American Century, 'Letter to President Clinton on Iraq', 26 January 1998: <http://www.newamericancentury.org/iraqclintonletter.htm>.

56 Khalilzad, 'Losing the moment?', p. 101.

57 'The National Security Strategy of the United States of America', September 2002, p. 3: <http://www.whitehouse.gov/nsc/nss1.html>.

58 Ibid.

59 Ibid., p. 27.

60 President George W. Bush, 'Preface letter', in 'The National Security Strategy of the United States', 17 September 2002, p. 1: <http://www.whitehouse.gov/nsc/nssintro.html>.
61 Ibid., p. 25.
62 Robert Kagan, 'The benevolent empire', *Foreign Policy*, 111, summer (1998), pp. 24–35, at p. 26.
63 This phrase is used repeatedly throughout the 'National Security Strategy of the United States'.
64 Ibid., p. 6.
65 President George W. Bush, 'President's remarks at the United Nations General Assembly', 12 September 2002, p. 2: <http://www.whitehouse.gov/news/releases/2002/09/20020912-1.html>.
66 'National Security Strategy', p. 13.

Chapter 2 The Alchemy of Power

1 William E. Connolly, *The Terms of Political Discourse*, 3rd edn (Princeton: Princeton University Press, 1993), p. 10.
2 Barry Hindess, *Discourses of Power: From Hobbes to Foucault* (Oxford: Blackwell, 1996), ch. 1.
3 Hans J. Morgenthau, *Politics Among Nations: The Struggle for Power and Peace*, 6th edn (New York: McGraw Hill, 1986), chs 7–10.
4 Hindess, *Discourses of Power*, p. 1.
5 Gerth and Mills (eds), *From Max Weber: Essays in Sociology* (London: Routledge & Kegan Paul, 1948), p. 78.
6 Robert O. Keohane and Joseph S. Nye, *Power and Interdependence*, 2nd edn (New York: Harper Collins, 1989), p. 44.
7 Thucydides, *History of the Peloponnesian War* (Harmondsworth: Penguin, 1972), pp. 401–2.
8 Robert W. Cox, 'Social forces, states, and world orders: beyond international relations theory', *Millennium: Journal of International Studies*, 10, 2 (1981), pp. 126–55, at p. 153.

9   Condoleezza Rice, 'Promoting the national interest', *Foreign Affairs*, 79, 1 (2000), pp. 45–62, at pp. 47, 49.

10 Charles Krauthammer, 'The unipolar moment', *Foreign Affairs*, 70, 1 (1990/91), pp. 23–33, at p. 24. Italics added.

11 Stephen D. Brooks and William Wohlforth, 'American primacy in perspective', *Foreign Affairs*, 81, 4 (2002), pp. 20–33, at p. 21.

12 Ibid., pp. 22–3.

13 'The National Security Strategy of the United States', September 2002: <http://www.whitehouse.gov/nsc/nss1.html> p. 3. Italics added.

14 Rice, 'Promoting the national interest', pp. 45–6.

15 Robert O. Keohane, *International Institutions and State Power: Essays in International Relations Theory* (Boulder, CO: Westview Press, 1989), p. 3.

16 Krauthammer, 'The unipolar moment', p. 25.

17 Rice, 'Promoting the national interest', p. 47.

18 Morgenthau, *Politics Among Nations*, p. 13.

19 Paul Kennedy, *The Rise and Fall of the Great Powers: Economic Change and Military Conflict from 1500 to 2000* (London: Unwin Hyman, 1988).

20 Brooks and Wohlforth, 'American primacy in perspective', pp. 23, 30–1.

21 Ibid., p. 32.

22 Ibid., p. 33.

23 Rice, 'Promoting the national interest', pp. 47, 49.

24 Josef Joffe, 'Who's afraid of Mr. Big?', *The National Interest*, 64, summer (2001), pp. 43–52, at p. 43.

25 Max Weber, *The Theory of Social and Economic Organization* (New York: Free Press, 1957), p. 152.

26 Joseph S. Nye. *The Paradox of American Power: Why the World's Only Superpower Can't Go it Alone* (Oxford: Oxford University Press, 2002), p. 4.

27 James C. Scott, *Domination and the Arts of Resistance* (New Haven: Yale University Press, 1990).

28 Anthony Giddens, *A Contemporary Critique of Historical Materialism: Volume One, Power, Property, and the State* (Berkeley, CA: University of California Press, 1981), p. 51.

29 Michel Crozier and Erhard Friedberg, *Actors and Systems: The Politics of Collective Action* (Chicago: University of Chicago Press, 1980), pp. 30–1.
30 Robert W. Jackman, *Power Without Force: The Political Capacity of Nation-States* (Ann Arbor: The University of Michigan Press, 1993), p. 30.
31 See David Beetham, *The Legitimation of Power* (London: Macmillan, 1991); Thomas Franck, *The Power of Legitimacy Among Nations* (New York: Oxford University Press, 1990); and Ian Hurd, 'Legitimacy and authority in international politics', *International Organization*, 53, 2, spring (1999), pp. 379–408.
32 Edmund Burke, 'On conciliation with the colonies', in *Speeches and Letters on American Affairs* (London: J. M. Dent and Sons, 1908), pp. 76–141.
33 Niccolò Machiavelli, *The Prince*, in *The Portable Machiavelli*, eds Peter Bondanella and Mark Musa (Harmondsworth: Penguin, 1979), pp. 13–146.
34 Charles Merriam, *Political Power: Its Composition and Incidence* (New York: McGraw Hill, 1934), p. 180.
35 Lisa Martin, 'The rational state choice of multilateralism', in *Multilateralism Matters: The Theory and Praxis of an Institutional Form*, ed. John Gerard Ruggie (New York: Columbia University Press, 1993), pp. 91–121.
36 Krauthammer, 'The unipolar moment', p. 25.
37 Alexander Wendt, *Social Theory of International Politics* (Cambridge: Cambridge University Press, 1999), ch. 6.
38 Anthony Giddens, *The Constitution of Society: Outline of the Theory of Structuration* (Berkeley, CA: University of California Press, 1984), p. 24.
39 Daniel Philpott, *Revolutions in Sovereignty* (Princeton: Princeton University Press, 2001), p. 12.
40 Christian Reus-Smit, *The Moral Purpose of the State: Culture, Social Identity, and Institutional Rationality in International Relations* (Princeton: Princeton University Press, 1999).
41 Krauthammer, 'The unipolar moment', p. 33.
42 Nye, *The Paradox of American Power*, p. 142.
43 Ibid., p. 9.

44 Robert Cox, 'Gramsci, hegemony, and international relations', in *Gramsci, Historical Materialism and International Relations*, ed. Stephen Gill (Cambridge: Cambridge University Press, 1993), p. 61.

45 Bruce Cronin, 'The paradox of hegemony: America's ambiguous relationship with the United Nations', *European Journal of International Relations*, 7, 1 (2001), pp. 103–30, at p. 103.

46 Ibid., p. 105.

47 Ibid., p. 111.

48 Francis Fukuyama, *The End of History and the Last Man* (New York: Free Press, 1992), pp. xviii–xx.

Chapter 3 The Real World

1 See Elizabeth Kier, *Imagining War: French and British Military Doctrine Between the Wars* (Princeton: Princeton University Press, 1997).

2 Ernest Renan, 'What is a nation?', in *Readings in World Politics*, ed. Robert Goldwin (New York: Oxford University Press, 1970), p. 409.

3 Robert Kagan, 'The benevolent empire', *Foreign Policy*, 111, summer (1998), pp. 24–35, at p. 26.

4 President George W. Bush, 'State of the Union Address 2003', 28 January 2003: <http://www.whitehouse.gov/news/releases/2003/03/20030128-19.html>.

5 Ibid.

6 Robert Kagan, 'Power and weakness', *Policy Review*, 113, June/July (2002), pp. 3–28, at p. 15.

7 President George W. Bush, 'Radio address to the nation', 1 March 2003: <http://www.whitehouse.gov/news/releases/2003/03/20030301.html>. Also see 'Remarks by the President at the American Enterprise Institute annual dinner', 26 February 2003: <http://www.whitehouse.gov/news/releases/2003/02/iraq/20030226-10.html>.

8 Chalmers Johnson, *Los Angeles Times*, 17 October 2002. Also see John Dower, *Warning from History: Don't Expect Democracy in Iraq*, Japan Policy Research Institute Occasional Paper No. 30 (Cardiff, CA: Japan Policy Research Institute, 2003).

9 For an excellent collection of different perspectives, see *Worlds in Collision: Terror and the Future of Global Order*, eds Ken Booth and Tim Dunne (London: Palgrave Macmillan, 2002).

10 Secretary of Defense Donald Rumsfeld, *Annual Report to the President and the Congress, 2002* (Washington, DC: Department of Defense, 2002), p. 10.

11 Ibid.

12 Christian Reus-Smit, *The Moral Purpose of the State: Culture, Social Identity, and Institutional Rationality in International Relations* (Princeton: Princeton University Press, 1999), ch. 6.

13 Hedley Bull, *The Anarchical Society: A Study of Order in World Politics*, 3rd edn (London: Palgrave Macmillan, 2002), pp. 9, 13.

14 Ibid., p. 13.

15 Ibid., p. 269.

16 Michael Barnett and Martha Finnemore, 'The politics, power, and pathologies of international organizations', *International Organization*, 53, 4 (1999), pp. 699–732.

17 <http://www.aei.org/events/eventID.329,filter.foreign/event_detail.asp>.

18 Charles Krauthammer, 'The unipolar moment', *Foreign Affairs*, 70, 1 (1990/91), pp. 23–33, at p. 33.

19 On the Bretton Woods institutions, see G. John Ikenberry, 'A world economy restored: expert consensus and the Anglo-American postwar settlement', *International Organization*, 46, 1, winter (1992), pp. 289–322.

20 Steve Weber, 'Shaping the postwar balance of power: multilateralism in NATO', in *Multilateralism Matters: The Theory and Praxis of an Institutional Form*, ed. John Gerard Ruggie (New York: Columbia University Press, 1993), p. 267.

21 Tzvetan Todorov, *The Conquest of America: The Question of the Other* (New York: Harper, 1992).

22 On Westphalia and Utrecht, see Reus-Smit, *The Moral Purpose of the State*; and Daniel Philpott, *Revolutions in Sovereignty* (Princeton: Princeton University Press, 2001). On the standard of civilization, see Gerrit W. Gong, *The Standard of 'Civilization' in International Society* (Oxford: Clarendon Press, 1984).

23 Christian Reus-Smit, 'Human rights and the social construction of sovereignty', *Review of International Studies*, 27, 4 (2001), pp. 519–38; and Robert H. Jackson, *Quasi-States: Sovereignty, International Relations, and the Third World* (Cambridge: Cambridge University Press, 1990).

24 Thomas J. Biersteker, 'The triumph of neoclassical economics in the developing world: policy convergence and bases of governance in the international economic order', in *Governance Without Government: Order and Change in World Politics*, eds James N. Rosenau and Ernst Otto Czempiel (Cambridge: Cambridge University Press, 1992), p. 106.

25 Charles Tilly, *Coercion, Capital, and European States: AD 990–1990* (Oxford: Blackwell, 1990), p. 4.

26 See 'Global poverty monitoring': <http://www.worldbank.org/research/povmonitor/>.

27 United Nations Development Program, *Human Development Report 2001: Making New Technologies Work for Human Development* (New York: Oxford University Press, 2001), pp. 22, 9.

28 Thomas Pogge, *World Poverty and Human Rights: Cosmopolitan Responsibilities and Reforms* (Cambridge: Polity, 2002), p. 98.

29 United Nations Development Program, *Human Development Report 2002: Deepening Democracy in a Fragmented World* (New York: Oxford University Press, 2002), p. 10.

30 United Nations Development Program, *Human Development Report 1999: Globalization with a Human Face* (New York: Oxford University Press, 1999), p. 3.

31 United Nations Environment Program, *Global Environment Outlook: 2000, Overview* (Nairobi: United Nations Environment Program, 1999), p. 15.

32 Ibid., p. 5.

33 Peter Christoff, 'Ecological modernization, ecological modernities', *Environmental Politics*, 5, 3 (1996), pp. 476–500; Maarten Hajer, *The Politics of Environmental Discourse: Ecological Modernization and the Policy Process* (Oxford: Clarendon Press, 1995); and Albert Weale, *The New Politics of Pollution* (Manchester: Manchester University Press, 1992).

34 Thomas F. Homer-Dixon, *Environment, Security, and Violence* (Princeton: Princeton University Press, 2001).

35 President George W. Bush, 'Graduation speech at West Point', 1 June 2002, p. 3: <http://www.whitehouse.gov/news/releases/2002/06/20020601-3>.

Chapter 4 The Ethics of Moralists

1 HandMade Films, *Monty Python's Life of Brian*. Copyright 1979, Python (Monty) Pictures Ltd.

2 Peter Kilfoyle, former Labour Defence Secretary, House of Commons Debate on Iraq, 18 March 2003: <http://news.bbc.co.uk/1/hi/uk_politics/2862325.stm>.

3 Niccolò Machiavelli, *The Discourses*, in *The Portable Machiavelli*, eds Peter Bondanella and Mark Musa (Harmondsworth: Penguin, 1979), p. 200.

4 President George W. Bush, 'State of the Union Address 2003', 28 January 2003: <http://www.whitehouse.gov/news/releases/2003/03/20030128-19.html>.

5 David C. Hendrickson, 'Toward universal empire: the dangerous quest for absolute security', *World Policy Journal*, 19, 3, fall (2002), pp. 1–10, at p. 9.

6 Thucydides, *History of the Peloponnesian War* (Harmondsworth: Penguin, 1972), pp. 401–2.

7 Mancur Olson, *The Logic of Collective Action: Public Goods and the Theory of Groups* (Cambridge, MASS: Harvard University Press, 1965), pp. 14–16.
8 Hedley Bull, *The Anarchical Society: A Study of Order in World Politics*, 3rd edn (London: Palgrave Macmillan, 2002), p. 199.
9 Ibid., p. 200.
10 Ibid., p. 93.
11 Olson, *The Logic of Collective Action*, p. 2.
12 Robert O. Keohane, *After Hegemony: Cooperation and Discord in the World Political Economy* (Princeton: Princeton University Press, 1984), p. 69.
13 Charles Kindleberger, *The World in Depression 1929–1939* (Harmondsworth: Penguin, 1973).
14 Joseph S. Nye, *The Paradox of American Power: Why the World's Only Superpower Can't Go it Alone* (Oxford: Oxford University Press, 2002), pp. 141–7.
15 Henry Shue, *Basic Rights: Subsistence, Affluence, and US Foreign Policy*, 2nd edn (Princeton: Princeton University Press, 1996).
16 Lea Brilmayer, *American Hegemony: Political Morality in a One-Superpower World* (New Haven: Yale University Press, 1994), p. 19.
17 Ibid., pp. 61–2.
18 Ibid., p. 220.
19 David Halloran Lumsdaine, *Moral Vision in International Politics: The Foreign Aid Regimes 1949–1989* (Princeton: Princeton University Press, 1993).
20 Jean-Jacques Rousseau, 'On social contract or the principles of political right', in *Rousseau's Political Writings*, eds Alan Ritter and Julia Conway Bonadella (New York: Norton, 1988), p. 88.
21 Bull, *The Anarchical Society*, p. 86.
22 Ibid., p. 91.
23 Hedley Bull, 'Justice in international relations: the 1983 Hagey lectures (1948)', in *Hedley Bull on International Society*, eds Kai Alderson and Andrew Hurrell (London: Macmillan, 2000), pp. 206–45.

24   John Rawls, *A Theory of Justice* (Oxford: Oxford University Press, 1971), p. 3.

25   Shue, *Basic Rights*, p. 19.

26   Christian Reus-Smit, 'The strange death of liberal international theory', *European Journal of International Law*, 12, 43, June (2001), pp. 573–93.

27   Bull, 'Justice in international relations', p. 227.

28   Charter of the United Nations, Article 39.

29   Richard Price, 'Reversing the gun sights: transnational civil society targets land mines', *International Organization*, 52, 3 (1998), pp. 575–612.

30   Margaret E. Keck and Kathryn Sikkink, *Activists Beyond Borders: Advocacy Networks in World Politics* (Ithaca, NY: Cornell University Press, 1998), p. 35.

31   See Nicholas Wheeler, *Saving Strangers: Humanitarian Intervention in International Society* (Oxford: Oxford University Press, 2001).

32   Michael Walzer, *Just and Unjust Wars: A Moral Argument with Historical Illustrations* (Harmondsworth: Penguin, 1977), p. 101. My definition differs from Walzer's in that I include starvation.

33   Henry Shue, 'Let whatever is smouldering erupt? Conditional sovereignty, reviewable intervention, and Rwanda 1994', in *Between Sovereignty and Global Governance*, eds Albert J. Paolini, Anthony P. Jarvis and Christian Reus-Smit (London: Macmillan, 1998), pp. 76–7.

34   International Commission on Intervention and State Sovereignty, *The Responsibility to Protect* (Ottawa: International Development Research Centre, 2001).

35   President George W. Bush, 'Graduation speech at West Point', 1 June 2002: <http://www.whitehouse.gov/news/releases/2002/06/20020601-3.html>.

36   Nicholas Lemann, 'Without a doubt', *Sydney Morning Herald Magazine, Good Weekend*, 15 February 2003, pp. 22–30.

37   Bush, 'Graduation speech at West Point'.

38 President George W. Bush, 'Radio address to the nation', 1 March 2003: <http://www.whitehouse.gov/news/releases/2003/03/20030301.html>.

39 President George W. Bush, 'Remarks by President at the American Enterprise Institute annual dinner', 26 February 2003: <http://www.whitehouse.gov/news/releases/2003/02/iraq/20030226–10.html>.

40 Rousseau, 'On social contract', p. 96.

41 'Going it alone', *The Bulletin of Atomic Scientists*, 58, 4, July/August (2002), pp. 36–7.

42 George Monbiot, 'One rule for them', the *Guardian*, 25 March 2003.

Chapter 5 Coercion and Exit

1 Charles Krauthammer, 'The unipolar moment revisited', *The National Interest*, 70, winter (2002/3), pp. 5–17, at p. 6.

2 Ibid., p. 7.

3 Ibid., p. 15.

4 Ibid., p. 12.

5 Ibid., p. 17.

6 Ibid.

7 Albert O. Hirschman, *Exit, Voice, and Loyalty: Responses to Decline in Firms, Organizations, and States* (Cambridge, MASS: Harvard University Press, 1970), p. 107.

8 Steven Weisman, 'A long, winding road to a diplomatic dead end', *New York Times*, 17 March 2003. A similar yet more strident critique of the Administration's diplomacy was published the same day in the *Washington Post*.

9 Paul Wolfowitz, 'Statement before the House National Security Committee', 18 September 1998: <http://www.newamericancentury.org/iraqsep1898.htm>.

10 Bob Woodward, *Bush at War* (New York: Simon and Schuster, 2002), p. 49.

11 President George W. Bush, 'President's remarks at the United Nations General Assembly', 12 September 2002:

<http://www.whitehouse.gov/news/releases/2002/09/ 20020912–1. html>.

12 Ibid.

13 Caroline Overington, 'Bush takes one step forward, and then two back', *Sydney Morning Herald*, 21–2 September 2002, p. 20.

14 United Nations Security Council Resolution 1441, paragraphs 2, 5, 12 and 13.

15 Bush, 'President's remarks at the United Nations General Assembly'.

16 Edward Gibbon, *The Portable Gibbon*, Dero A. Saunders (Harmondsworth: Penguin, 1955), p. 621. My emphases.

17 Thucydides, *History of the Peloponnesian War* (Harmondsworth: Penguin, 1972), Book I.144, p. 122.

18 Ibid., Book VII.87, pp. 536–7.

Index